P9-CEV-154

7/92

THE
COLOUR
OF CANADA

THE
COLOUR
OF CANADA

text by

HUGH MACLENNAN

The Canadian Illustrated Library

Contents

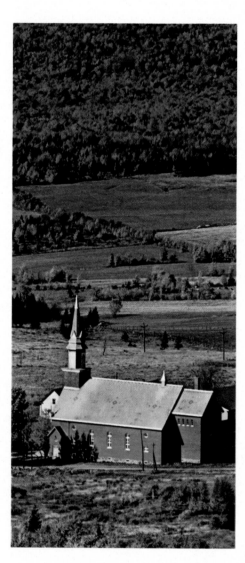

A journey across Canada in words and pictures

FIRST EDITION
© Copyright 1967
McClelland and Stewart Limited

REVISED EDITION
© Copyright 1972
McClelland and Stewart Limited

ALL RIGHTS RESERVED
No part of this book may be
reproduced in any form
without written permission
from the publishers,
excepting brief quotations
for review purposes.

THE CANADIAN ILLUSTRATED LIBRARY

McClelland & Stewart Limited
The Canadian Publishers
ILLUSTRATED BOOKS DIVISION
25 Hollinger Road, Toronto 374

0-7710-0031-6

Prologue

The first edition of this book appeared early in 1967 and was intended as a testimonial to our Centennial Year. We never expected that the demand for it would outlast 1967, but for five years the demand has been constant. These have been long years for all of us and the psychic and political shiftings both in Canada and the rest of the world have been dramatic. A new edition of this book is essential if it still professes to give a sense of the colour of Canada.

How much has happened since that spring afternoon in 1967 when Expo 67 was unveiled in Montreal! Nature itself shone on us that day. The air was crisp, the wind-scoured sky was cloudless, beneath it the St. Lawrence flowed as blue as the Athabasca and the fields beyond the river were as green as Ireland. On the river islands Expo 67, that perfect melding of French-Canadian flair and Anglo-Canadian practicality, marriage unique between art and technology, seemed to be holding its breath. Here at last was the outward and visible symbol of what Canada could not yet believe she had become.

One by one the flags of the visiting nations rose on their standards in La Place des Nations and were broken free, the name of each of them ringing out like a bell. The whole world seemed to be there. Finally the name "Canada" was spoken, the new Maple Leaf flag went up and instantly a squadron of R.C.A.F. planes cracked over in salute and burst upward like a fan of rockets into the blue. Up jetted Expo's fountains and I was one of the thousands who felt the lump in the throat. Beside me was my oldest living friend who happened also to be Canada's Auditor-General (he must have spent many a day and night worrying about the cost of all this to the tax-payer) and I saw his eyes suddenly shine. He pounded my back and cried, "My God, we've made it! We've made it after all!"

So indeed it seemed in the halcyon days of May, June and July. So extraordinary was the spirit of Expo that the neighbouring pavilions of Israel and Egypt remained unruffled even during the Six Days' War. Meanwhile all over the land Canadians were celebrating the hundredth birthday of a nation neither the British nor the Americans, nor for that matter too many Canadians themselves, had believed would endure longer than a decade or two. Looking over the national flags assembled there I thought again how ironic history is. Among those 62 visiting nations from all the world's continents only sixteen were politically older than Canada and of these famous veterans, which ones could claim to have been more fortunate?

France was enduring her Second Empire when Canada was born; now she had her Fifth Republic. The Empire on which the sun never set until 1941 had shrunk to the little United Kingdom which soon would abandon nine centuries of stupendously creative isolation and rejoin the continent to which she had originally been attached by Claudius Caesar some two decades after the crucifixion of Christ. The Russia which had been a Czarist agrarian despotism in 1867 was now a communist technological despotism. How many revolutions had Mexico suffered since Canada's birth? How many Greece,

Venezuela and Cuba? Austria had shrunk from Europe's greatest land-empire into a tiny state centered on ancient Vienna. Belgium had twice been invaded and occupied; the Netherlands, Denmark, Norway, Greece, Abyssinia and Siam once invaded and occupied. Japan had convulsed the world, been bombed to the verge of extinction, had recovered astonishingly. Among these politically older nations, which ones had been so consistently fortunate as ourselves? Only Sweden, Switzerland and the United States.

But even then the tocsins were ringing in Canada and they still are. Five years ago I wrote in the first edition of this book that "I can't give myself the illusion of being sure of many things anymore. Certain facts, knowledges, observations and intuitions – armed and often confused by these, one lives in a world almost but not quite out of human control, its accumulated information so vast that the most learned of men know they are ignorant, its technical communications so efficient that it has been called an electronic village, the new phrase for a technologically created Babel". (Since then Telstar has gone into orbit) "We try to come to terms with material power such as there never was, matched by an individual uncertainty of soul unparalleled since the Black Death. A new age is a-borning, it is probably here. But nobody I have met or read understands it and not many even pretend to."

Now I must write a strange sentence. We are in the beginning of the first post-Christian Era, yet there are signs everywhere that the spirit of Christ is nearer to men than it has been for centuries.

Also within these past five years man has made what is probably the most important discovery of his entire career as a species. He has finally found his own true origin. Modern scientific dating applied to a fossil turned up in Africa indicates that we creatures of the big brain, we *homines sapientes sapientes*, have a full-fledged human ancestry which cannot be much older than twenty thousand years. "Wonders are many," sang the chorus in *Antigone*, "but the greatest wonder is man. . . . Cunning beyond fancy's dreams is the fertile skill which brings him, now to evil, now to good."

These lines of Sophocles could serve as a theme song for the five years which followed 1967. The great leader who saved France from revolution came to Expo, according to himself with sincere goodwill to all, in order to help a revolution happen here. The Canada which shone so brightly in 1967 sank into the squalid darkness of political kidnapping and murder only three years later. An astounding nexus of technology landed two teams of astronauts on the moon, whence they departed leaving behind them a little plastic *Stars And Stripes* to remind the Creator that Kilroy was there, too. Here on our old earth technology is now admitted, as was not the case five years ago, so to have polluted the air, the waters and the cities that unless it changes its ways it will succeed in collapsing the biosphere. Five years ago Canada wished to recognize Communist China but did not do so for fear of affronting the United States. Five years later Richard Nixon, who had spent a long career denouncing as traitors all who even contemplated a recognition of Mainland China, went to Peking in person and saw to it that the whole world watched his performance over television.

Nixon's about-face may well be another proof that there really does exist a fail-safe mechanism in species which prevents any species from destroying itself totally, whatever it may do to other species. All sane men must be thankful that Nixon went to China. But this otherwise laudable change in American foreign policy is sure to confront Canada with the greatest challenge of her national existence.

Whenever a great empire suffers a total strategic defeat in war the whole world rocks, and a total strategic defeat is what the United States has suffered in Viet Nam. Not all the political camouflage thrown up by the media can hide one staring fact: in the far East the United States has been repulsed after more than a century during which she has been steadily thrusting her commercial, po-

litical and military power into that area. Just as the Roman Empire found it could go no farther into Germany than the Rhine, so the United States has found she can penetrate no farther into Asia than her base-islands in the Western Pacific. Just as the Roman *imperium* was compelled to fall back upon herself and her client states in western Europe, North Africa and the Middle East, so now does the American *imperium* (though fortunately "empire" is not yet an entirely clean word in the United States) fall back upon the heartland of its home continent. President Nixon had not been home from China for more than ten days before his Secretary of State announced that the United States intends to concentrate its efforts much more heavily than before on Latin America and Canada.

What this will mean eventually for Canada is anyone's guess, but it is nobody's guess – we all know it – that the United States has always been a catalyst in Canadian affairs. Never before have her power-men been so interested in us as they are now. For over a century Canadians have emigrated into the United States and very few Americans settled here. But during the past five years thousands of Americans have been emigrating into Canada and not all of them have come to escape the military draft. Many have come to escape the pollution, and over-crowding, the racial strife and the general over-organization of their native land. But the essential power structure of our neighbour is still in total control and we watch it and wonder what it really intends. We ask ourselves whether sheer pressure of events will compel it to consolidate a kind of Fortress Western Hemisphere in which computer-science will combine with the multinational American corporations to homogenize the entire New World – as it was called only yesterday before it grew old without ever having really grown up.

If this is to become the policy of the United States, will it mean that Canada is destined to be absorbed and disappear from history at the very moment when she has become mature enough to make an original contribution to it?

Another question-mark. So perhaps this is the time to switch back to the gist of my original text of five years ago, which may be more urgently applicable to the Canada of the mid '70's than it was to the Canada of 1967.

Any nation (as distinct from an empire) is ultimately held together by its land, its territory. Most of the pictures in this book are of a Canadian land which is far vaster than any one man can hope to comprehend. It still contains a small nation even though Canada's population today is larger than Britain's in the year of Waterloo. The land will endure as long as the world does, though in what condition will depend upon humanity, yet in the long term the nation is only a tenant on it.

How long the present tenant's lease will run is going to depend upon much more than the nation's present inhabitants. This land is rich and magnificent. After the climate warmed up (lately it is cooling off again) it became much more attractive than it was two centuries ago when Voltaire dismissed it as *quelques arpents de neige*. Everyone knows that the world is now disastrously overcrowded and that the rights of small nations weigh little against hunger, greed, power and the need for living space. However, at the moment the land is still presumed to belong to those who live on it.

In a way, this nation is a miracle of illogicality and nothing is more miraculous about her than her stubborn survival despite the continuous efforts of pundits and businessmen to prove that her survival makes no sense. How often have we heard the reasons — no sense economically, politically, geographically or culturally. She makes no sense, they say. Neither does a giraffe. She is not a logical construction. She never was, and I have the idea that if she ever tries to be logical about herself she will rationalize herself out of existence. As early as 1963, French Canadian separatists had selected the Centennial Year as the logical one for Canada's dissolution. But at the same time Mayor Jean Drapeau went straight ahead and won Expo 67 for Mont-

real. So it has always been, for political unity as it is understood elsewhere seems the last thing the Canadian people want, though most of them assert that it is our greatest need. Is this logical? Obviously not, and that's fine with me, for if logic is ever carried to its final extreme in human affairs, what does it lead to but insanity? Psychotics are nearly always logical, neurotics never are. But neurotics are at least sane.

"*Il est bon,*" wrote a French philosopher, "*et plus souvent qu'on ne le pense, de savoir de n'avoir pas de l'esprit.*" A good thing not to be intelligent? The whole spirit of our century laughs at such an idea. It has bet the bankroll on intelligence. It trusts it so much it has even invented a mechanical brain.

Yet it is a plain fact that many a plain man has been asking for some time what good the superbrains of our century have been doing for humanity. Poor old Einstein's genius led straight to the H-bomb. Hot wars and cold wars, nuclear weapons with miraculous vehicles to deliver them, revolutions and counter-revolutions, rising unemployment combined with rising inflation, laws intended to make us free and secure imprisoning us in strangling bureaucracies, propaganda and Madison Avenue, a super-colossal technology harnessed to produce the one condition of life which man has always found intolerable — leisure. The most brilliant and energetic intellects of our age have occupied themselves with these accomplishments to the virtual exclusion of everything else.

But Canada is not a brilliant nation and one of the few things which seem reasonably clear to me, if to nobody else, is that by pure instinct (there can be no other explanation) we are more strongly than ever asserting the historic decision of our ancestors to stand as aloof as we can from the obsessions and drives of our mighty and (I hope) still friendly neighbour. We have even been saying this publicly lately as hardly any of us did five years ago, but just how aloof we can be is one of those nice calculations so dear to the Canadian soul: all the American investment we can get though not too much American investment; economic union with the United States but not necessarily economic union; all the American university teachers who can't get jobs in their own country must be permitted to take jobs here, but not too many American university teachers; all possible bilingualism and bi-culturalism, but not too much bilingualism and bi-culturism. O Canada, with such subtleties as these we stand on guard for thee!

We all know that the Canadian nation – informal questionnaires put by myself to McGill undergraduates satisfy me that at least 9% of us know it – came into being because our ancestors repudiated the most important single event in the history of the western hemisphere, the American Revolution. Canada exists today because they said no to that. She will cease to exist if she ever says yes to that, unless she does so in the spirit of a girl in the back seat of a taxi with one eye on the meter and the other on the profile of the determined man who took her out that night.

Just the same, that decision of our ancestors has haunted their descendants ever since. The United States has been quite the most marvellous country in the world. She became so rich, successful, exciting and proud, and for years her public pleasure in herself was an enchantment. The ideals on which she was founded rang like bugles around the globe. Her techniques were copied everywhere, and in no countries more meticulously than in Canada and the Soviet Union.

No wonder the descendants of the original Loyalists, looking enviously across the border the British had so negligently agreed to accept for them, asked themselves whether their ancestors had not ruined their children's lives by betting them on the wrong horse. Even some French Canadians thought the same. Calixa Lavalée, the author of our national anthem, was one of them. He left Canada, became an American citizen and from New York sent pamphlets home urging his former countrymen to follow his example. Nor was there ever a lack of those who did. Successive genera-

tions were depleted by hundreds of thousands – millions would be no exaggeration – of energetic and able men and women who gravitated like iron filings to the magnet and were lost to Canada.

Nearly everyone called Canada negative in her growing years, and so she was. The only way it seemed possible for French Canada to survive was to make Quebec a virtual reservation, repudiating the value of nearly everything that had happened since 1763. English Canada clung with pathetic loyalty to the fading glories of a Britain that had little interest in her except in time of war or a royal visit. Worse was yet to come. In the twentieth century the final death of the British Empire coincided with the swamping of our information-media by those of the United States, and the old frustation of the baffled horse-player changed into a kind of guilt-neurosis, as though by staying Canadians (and therefore not being Americans) we were defying the will of God. For the Americans were serious when they called the United States "God's Own Country." They still are. "The tremendous prosperity, power and blessing," wrote Billy Graham, "which America has enjoyed through the years came because we as a nation honoured God. It is, I believe, a direct fulfilment of the promise, 'Blessed is the nation whose God is the Lord.'"

But with stubborn negation, often against their conscious minds, the majority of us shied away from Manifest Destiny even after we had been trained to judge our worth solely as we saw it reflected in the eyes of our neighbours. This meant that whenever we boasted about anything, we boasted about our real estate, raw materials, wheat, scenery and Mounted Police, these being the only things Canadian that interested our neighbours. Until, perhaps, recently.

Our destiny, so we were told occasionally by our more optimistic politicians, always lay in some distant future and never was defined. Sir Wilfrid Laurier uttered the famous prediction that just as the nineteenth century had belonged to the United

States, so would the twentieth belong to Canada. Bold statements of this sort are so rare in Canada that this particular one found its way into most of our school books, though anyone who took a good look at it must have known how absurd it was. The nineteenth century never "belonged" to the United States; if it belonged to anyone it belonged to Britain, which cashed in during those years on her victory over France and her headstart in the Industrial Revolution. As for the twentieth century, from 1914 until the first Russian sputnik it clearly "belonged" to the United States, which cashed in on the decline of Europe and her own brilliance in business and technology. But the twentieth century is not over yet. Possibly, though in a sense very different from the one intended by Laurier, at least some of it may be shared by Canada if we have the nerve to follow the instinct of the nation's founders and translate it into a rational purpose.

A nation can become valuable to mankind only if it succeeds in co-operating with what might be called an historical need. For the first time Canada may have a chance of doing that. If we can resolve our own confusions here at home, we will have done more than make Canada a happier and more fruitful country than she is now. We will have set an example to other peoples confused and battered, pulled hither and thither by the struggle and obsessions of the two super-powers.

Let's look backward and ask ourselves frankly what actually were the reasons why the original Canadians repudiated the American Revolution. To understand them might help us make up our minds today. The usual explanations are that the Loyalists were Tories hostile to liberty and progress, while the French Canadian Church abominated democracy worse than the Vatican used to abominate Communism. But surely these explanations are superficial. Why should a French Canada abandoned by such a miserable practicing Catholic as Louis xv, owing neither him nor France an adulterated *sou*, the Union Jack of their conquerors flying over British

garrisons in their own cities, have said no to the Americans when they revolted against Britain? The reason was basic; it was not intelligent but visceral. They wanted to survive *as a people*, and it was as simple as that. If they said yes to the Revolution, they would prosper more as individuals in their material lives, but as a people they would disappear and lose all sense of themselves as such.

Why did the Loyalists, most of whom deplored the stupidity and corruption of Lord North's government, refuse to join the Revolution? Certainly not because they were anti-democratic or afraid of losing their privileges. Very few of them were rich and privileged, and if they had been hostile to democracy they never would have introduced the town meeting into Ontario and the Maritime Provinces, nor would their sons have struggled for responsible government in British North America until, without a revolution or severing their ties with the motherland, they won it.

What does all this mean unless it means that what the French Canadians and the Loyalists were rejecting was something deeper than was visible on the surface? Letters and statements made by Loyalists suggest that they knew very well what it was. It was not the ideals of the Revolution, but the hidden passions which those ideals masked.

In a famous book written in 1923 (*Studies In Classic American Literature*) D. H. Lawrence writes with a wild and fascinated eloquence about those drives which lay hidden underneath the idealism of the American Revolution, and few learned Americans have denied that he was basically right, especially in recent years when they have to live with the results of them.

Lawrence sought to explain the startling contradiction between the pride and confidence taken by Americans in their wonderful, rationally created nation and the violence, irrationality and unhappiness that have pervaded most of the best American literature from Melville and Hawthorne until the present day. The typical American hero of the deepest American literature is nearly always a

"The vastness is deceptive...only 7% could ever be cultivated"

Attungala, a Canadian citizen, strides through the
normal winter ground drift in the arctic highlands.

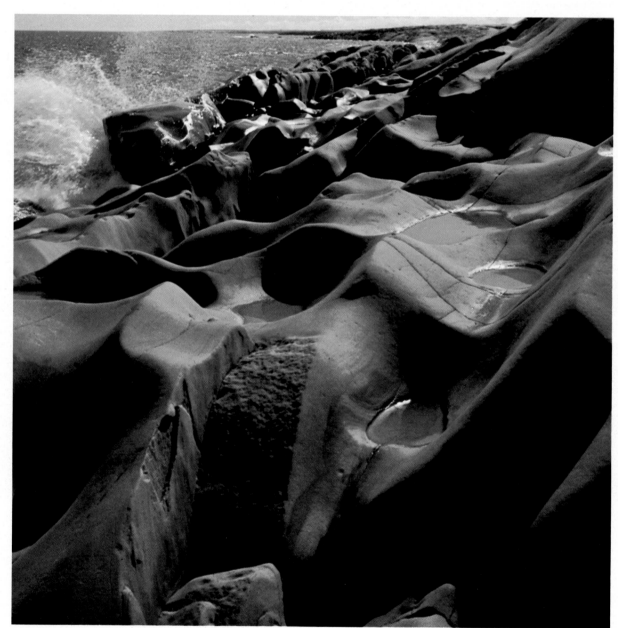

Soft rock formations on the west coast of Hudson Bay are sculptured and polished by the endless waves and shifting ice.

defeated *individual*, a desperate man alienated from the triumphant crowd: Captain Ahab striking his harpoons into the whale that symbolized the super-ego of American puritanism and the *Pequod* going down with flag flying, sunk by that same whale which here symbolizes the natural world which the conscious ego had tried to master; the lone American caught by the sheriff's posse and growling, "My name it is Sam Hall and I hate you one and all – God damn your eyes!" and now, in most post-war literature, the defiant American hero has merged into the passive anti-hero who can imagine no other role than civil disobedience. Why all this?

Lawrence finds his explanation in the hidden compulsions of many early New Englanders; had he been more familiar with literature south of the Mason and Dixon Line he would have found examples even more striking. Most of the revolutionary Americans, so Lawrence thought, were seeking to escape, to get away. But from what? The ineffectual authority of an ineffectual king who lived in London? And if there was a determination to create a state where all men would enjoy life, liberty and the pursuit of happiness, why did the revolutionaries retain the institution of slavery? Underneath the perfect rationality of the most perfect constitution lurked something hidden, and it was this that the Loyalists rejected.

Lawrence is right, surely, when he says that what America really sought to escape was nothing less than the human past of Europe – history itself and the long and exhausting burden of it. Under God in a new continent, they aspired to create a new and purer nation, uncontaminated by the evil past, free forever from the repetitive patterns of history and injustice. "No foreign entanglements" was echoed a century and a quarter later by Henry Ford's "History is bunk."

But nobody can escape from his past, neither can any nation live alone and escape from history, as successive American presidents have discovered. The effort to be superior to the past, superior to human nature, is more than human nature can bear, no matter how nobly people try to bear it. As Lawrence saw it, such an effort was bound to alienate the individual, the blood-and-flesh woman and man, and at the same time exalt and magnify the state which, as its power grew, imperceptibly was given the kind of worship and obedience usually offered to God. "Hear ye, O America, our nation is one nation" – and in order to preserve the mystique of its unity, the most humble and merciful of presidents waged the most terrible civil war in history. Now challenged by a newer messianic ideology, the power and concentration of the state has become . . . but these are deep waters, and we have no fishing rights in them.

But we still do have our huge country and our little nation. Nor is it anti-American to emphasize that it was because Canadians had no wish to alienate themselves from the past and from their European source that the Canadian nation came into being.

Earlier I said that this peculiar nation of ours, in most things important, acts from instinct and sentiment. She has always tried to guard her continuities. If to do so is unfashionable, her leaders pay unfailing lip-service to the pressures of the moment, but in practice they seek to guard the continuities. Why else was there such a soul-searching over the ditching of the Red Ensign in favour of a distinctive national flag? Why else does Quebec insist upon the maintenance of her French culture? Our instinct – perhaps in the insanity of the post-war years our reason goes along with it – tells us now that the only "unity" worth having is one which will permit the greatest possible variety of individual and collective differences, that the individual will have a chance only if he is given priority over the vast, impersonal state. The world today is on a psychic hinge, and the young generation, confused though it is, everywhere recognizes that the challenge it faces in the Age of Affluence is not a material but a spiritual one. Flesh and blood against the abstraction; genuine human needs against the needs of the super-organization.

"A land larger than any one person can hope to comprehend"

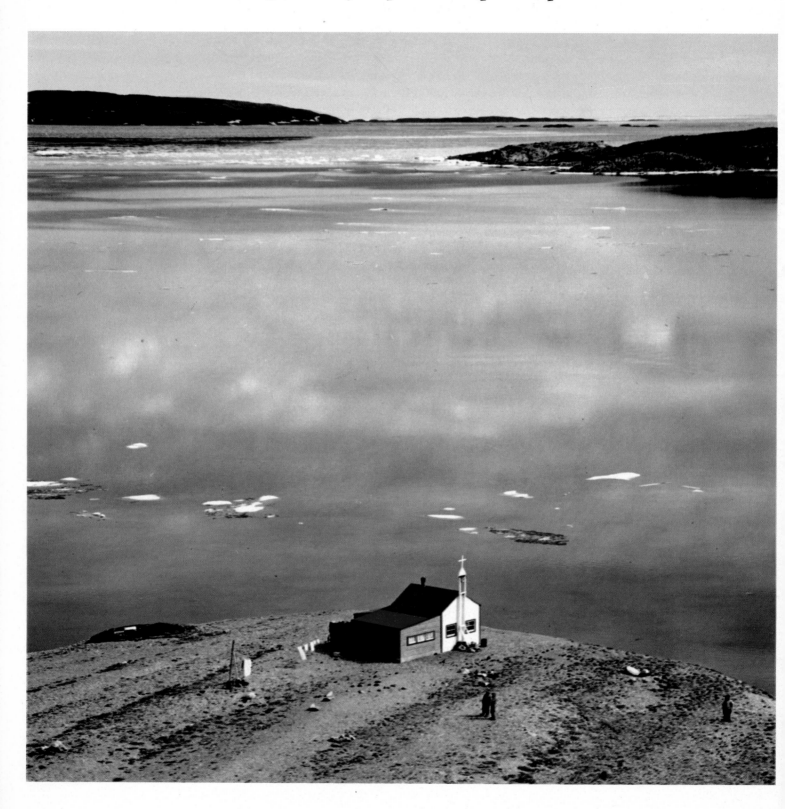

The Oblate church at Thom Bay, Northwest Territories.

Therefore I believe that the perennial Canadian "racial" problem is our greatest single asset. Again and again it has prevented us from opting for the kind of unity which turns a government into a huge abstraction. In our own muddled way we are still trying to provide in Canada a political home for diversity. Our two solitudes may still be solitary, but they have begun to talk with one another. Is it still wishful-thinking to believe that if Canada succeeds, she will be a pilot-plant for a broader human liberty in this frightened world? Could anything be worse for the over-burdened United States than to have us inflict our problems upon it?

We still have the land; we are still its tenants. The land is our overwhelming common denominator. A land of dramatic contrasts with an undeveloped frontier – much of it probably undevelopable – almost as large as Europe: great rivers, only a few of them polluted so far; thousands of lakes and three oceans flanking the whole. Stupidly, we overcrowd three urban areas, a buck being still sacred with us. But the plane which leaves Vancouver air terminal flies over virgin mountains within ten or fifteen minutes. The cars streaming out of Montreal and Toronto can usually reach the wilderness in less than two hours. When you stand on a high point in Quebec City you can see only a few miles away the ramparts of the Laurentian Shield.

This land is far more important than we are. To know it is to be young and ancient all at once. Its virginity is our visible link with the beginnings of the race and the millions of New Canadians who have come here have found constant reminders of their homes in older countries.

In 1937 when I went through Scandinavia to Russia, I said in Denmark, "But this is like Prince Edward Island"; in Sweden, "How like New Brunswick this is!" In Finland, "Just like Quebec fifteen miles north of the river, or Ontario above Simcoe." In Russia and Poland I thought inevitably of the prairie provinces. A few years ago, sailing from Athens along the coast of Argolis, had I not known I was in the Aegean I could easily have mistaken that rocky shore for the coasts of Cape Breton or Newfoundland. British Columbia is our Norway. And one dawn on the Mackenzie, waking in the wheelhouse of a dredge moored at Wrigley Harbour, the sun striking like a searchlight across the river under a mass of clouds, wild ducks and geese arrowing off the water – this was North America when the first white men saw it!

In this book we discover Canada somewhat as the explorers, settlers, and *voyageurs* discovered it. We begin at the rocky harbours of Newfoundland and Nova Scotia, glance at the gentle farmland of Prince Edward Island in summer and winter, at the old Loyalist city of Saint John and some of the lovely rivers of New Brunswick. We come to Gaspé, go up the St. Lawrence past modern Quebec and Montreal, enter briefly the Eastern Townships, then pass through the water gap leading to the Great Lakes and Ontario. We look at the new Toronto and a variety of scenes in Ontario before leaping across the Shield to the Prairies – space apparently limitless under shifting skies all the way to the Rocky Mountains. We go through the mountains to the coast where a sea bird flies out from the land over the Pacific. The North is still a separate region so far as communications and the life of the people are concerned, and we treat it separately in the pictures in this book.

Geographically, Canada consists of five very different regions: first, the Atlantic provinces, glacier-scraped, settled for the most part along the coasts (and in New Brunswick along the rivers), apparently small yet so indented that the coastline of "little" Nova Scotia is some 5,000 miles long – a distance much greater than an air line from Halifax to Victoria; then the nation's core, Quebec-Ontario, bound together despite linguistic differences by the St. Lawrence and Ottawa river systems and the Laurentian Shield; then the Prairies, a sea of land lying between the American border and the arbitrary line of the Northwest Territories; then the Cordilleran West; finally the North. This latter region consists of more than the Yukon, the North-

Colourful vegetation grows in rich profusion
in the valleys and on the hillsides of the
Artic north.

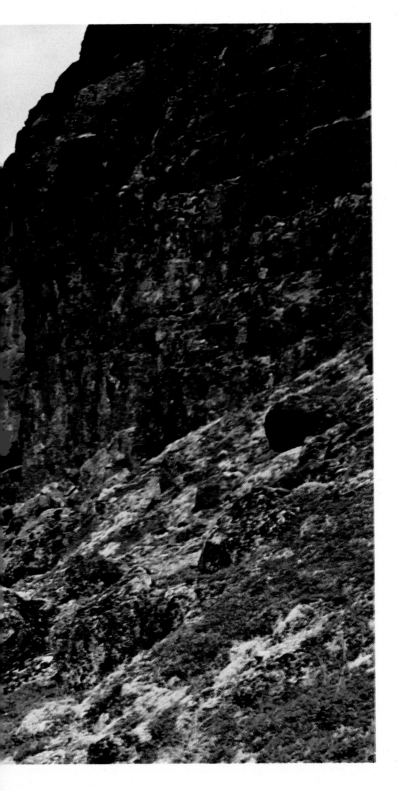

west Territories and the islands of the Arctic Ocean; along Hudson Strait, Ungava Bay, northern Labrador it overlaps Quebec and Newfoundland.

Canada's geographical vastness is deceptive. At the moment little more than 4% of the whole country is under cultivation; it has been estimated that only 7% ever can be. If the present trend continues, this will become a country where, apart from the Prairies, the population will be congregated in a number of densely populated areas suitable for trade and industry; in short a culture of cities like a colossal ancient Greece, with nature picturesque and largely unspoiled just outside them, a country as different as could be imagined from the United States with its rich parklands and thousands of small market towns.

Five years ago most Canadians seemed to welcome this prospect, but now it is beginning to seem somewhat horrible. Now we know at last that urban giantism in some regions of the United States has passed the point of no return. It breeds crime and frustration everywhere and it is no wonder that thousands of Americans in the last few years have been buying Canadian shore and forest land to escape from the concrete jail of modern megalopis. Will Canada move toward decentralization in the next few decades or will her cities develop into a cancer growth? I don't know.

But no matter what the population development, the contrast between the geographical and human maps of Canada will be startling for a long time to come, and this can be seen if we compare the present Canada to Great Britain.

The land area of the main British island is some 5,000 square miles smaller than that of the combined Atlantic provinces; the British population is 30 times greater. Quebec-Ontario is eleven times larger than Britain; the population is only a quarter as large. The Prairies exceed Britain in area by a ratio of 6.5 to 1; Britain's population exceeds theirs by 20 to 1. The corresponding ratios of land and population in British Columbia and the North are, respectively, 4-1 and 1-45; 16.5-1 and 1-250!

It has often been estimated that by the year 2,000 A.D. the total Canadian population will touch 40 millions, but we make no predictions about that here, remembering that in 1930 the experts predicted that by 1960 the population of the United States would level off at 145 millions. The present population explosion can easily be arrested in the Western nations and already there are indications that a falling-off has begun. Nowhere has this falling-off been more startling than in Quebec. Only twenty years ago the French Canadian birthrate was one of the highest in the western world; today, with the decline in religion, it has shrunk to the lowest in Canada. The only prediction we make here is that the central Mackenzie Basin will be more heavily populated than it is now; the country is beautiful and the mean temperatures in the region of Fort Simpson are higher than they were at Quebec a century ago. If mosquitos and blackflies can be controlled, this would be one of the finest lands anyone could wish.

A culture of cities with unspoiled nature in abundance, more fresh air and water than in any other part of the earth – if only our imaginations could look both back and forward, back to the loveliness of the cities of ancient Greece and forward to what such a combination of urbanity and the wilderness promises us! If only, instead of multiplying urban high rises, our city developers had the wisdom of Sir Christopher Wren, and kept the buildings lower and seeded the cities with parks!

Yet finally we seem to be saying yes to this land the ancient navigators discovered for us and the *voyageurs* opened up for us. Changes in the climate have made it easier for us than for the pioneers, but it still is a dramatic climate. If it becomes soft and tropical it is never for long. A storm breaks and astringent air pours in from the north to blow away the smog we still believe is allowable because there is temporary profit in it for those who make it. The sky is electric blue and old men remember their youth. This land is too precious to be put at auction.

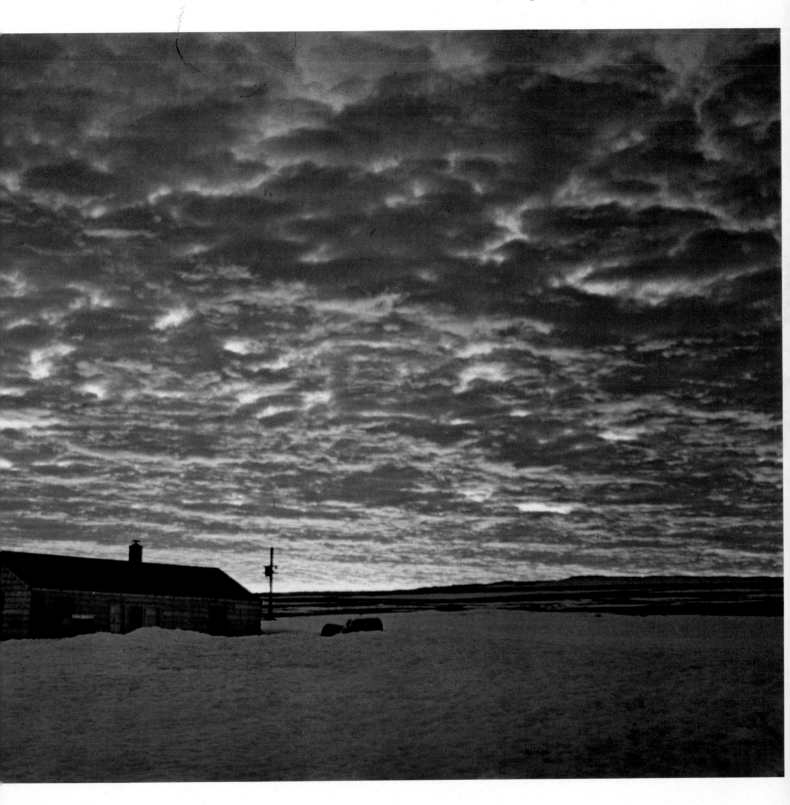

Midnight in May near the Arctic Circle.

The journey begins:

The Maritimes

Look at the art of the sea, how it shapes and
polishes granite. Feel its cold cleanness; its power
when it thunders against the land in a whole
gale. If you stood on the rocks of Peggy's Cove on
a day like this you would be in danger. If the
camera had been turned inland you would see spume
like thin snow rushing across a rising moor
of stunted trees with granite tors standing like
prehistoric monsters. Just behind this rock lies
the famous cove with little fishing boats,
jetties piled with lobster pots, white cottages and
a church. On fine days you can sit here in the
sun with your back propped against North America
and your eyes ranging over a sea that extends
uninterrupted to old Guyenne and Gascony.

OPPOSITE: PEGGY'S COVE, NOVA SCOTIA

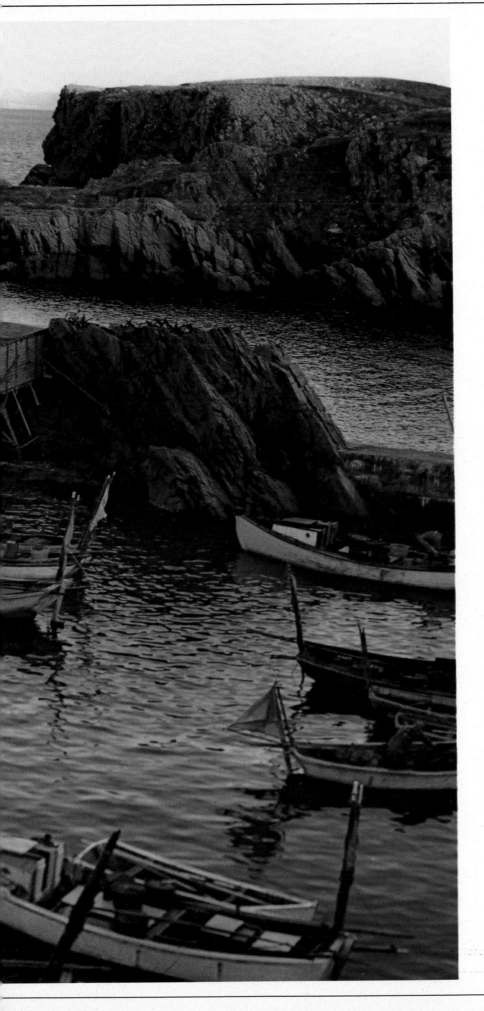

A tiny outport in Newfoundland where
men of the Caucasian race have
lived in the New World longer than
anywhere above the Rio Grande
or below the Spanish Main. Poetic
names, haunting or majestic,
redolent of history: Heart's Content,
Seldom-Come-By, Blow-Me-Down
(a corruption of Blomidon, the old
navigator), Port Aux Basques
(here Basque fishermen dried their
catches before taking them home);
Bonavista Bay, Conception Bay,
Placentia Bay, Avalon. Only a few years
ago in these regions people spoke
in the accents of Shakespeare's England.

Newfoundland has been always a
stepping stone between the
hemispheres. Vikings were here before
Cabot; Englishmen, Frenchmen,
Spaniards, Portuguese shared the
fishing rights before the
Pilgrims landed in Massachusetts.
The Labrador Current washes
the island, makes it chilly and foggy;
the storms are terrifying.
Steamers following the Great Circle
from New York to Europe pass
in sight of Cape Race, and the Titanic
was only the most famous of
the ones that failed to finish the voyage.
In little boats like these
the fishermen of Newfoundland put out
to the rescue in North Atlantic
winter gales. Alcock and Brown left
Newfoundland in 1919 on the
first non-stop trans-Atlantic flight.
In the Hitler War, Gander
was the last airport of Ferry Command.
Now, after centuries of heroic
isolation, Newfoundland is part of
Canada, and the continent,
the oldest and newest province.

HIBBS' HOLE, NEWFOUNDLAND

25

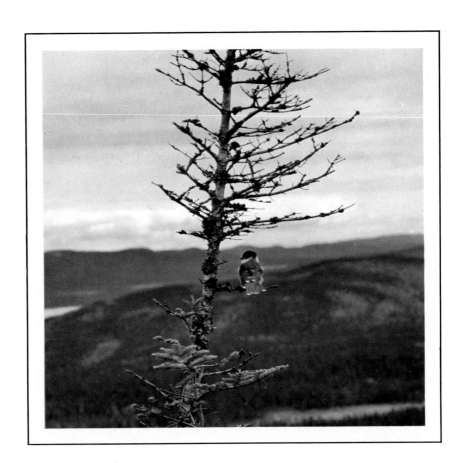

St. John's wind-swept, rain-washed houses — warm and comfortable, wonderful houses to grow up in like those of Saint John, N.B., today and of Halifax before Halifax lifted its face after the Hitler War. The finest wines drunk in North America are drunk in St. John's. Here, too, is played some of North America's shrewdest politics — politics can only be real where people know each other in the bones and the blood corpuscles, otherwise they are illusions called "images." A city that a while ago was almost a city-state. It was from Signal Hill in St. John's that Marconi sent his first trans-Atlantic wireless message. It was here, too, that Premier Joey Smallwood broke the last Family Compact in North America.

TERRA NOVA NATIONAL PARK, NEWFOUNDLAND

LEFT: ST. JOHN'S, NEWFOUNDLAND

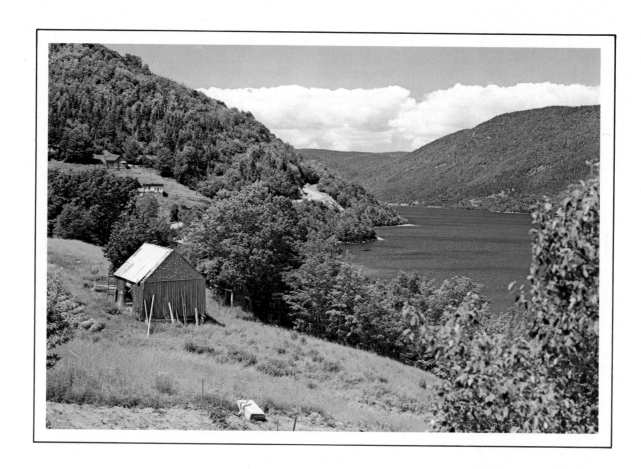

The ancient sea still washes the Maritimes, but almost gone is the life when the sea and the small family farms nourished the people. Less than a century ago Maritimers built, sailed and manned one-fifth of the merchant fleets of the entire world. The Cunard and White Star Lines were born here. But modern technology doomed both them and the old life-pattern. Now thousands of shore lots have been bought cheap by foreigners desperate to escape the hideousness that made their cities rich.

INGONISH FERRY, NOVA SCOTIA

Bogs, swamps, and second growth timber — often stunted from exposure to the ocean winds blasts — are found all along the shore as the land recovers from the effects of ancient glaciers which stripped away trillions of tons of soil exposing bare rock, and from the more recent effects of human settlement — especially logging operations and forest fires. The settlement area is the centre of much bird and animal life of the region.

CAPE BRETON ISLANDS, NOVA SCOTIA

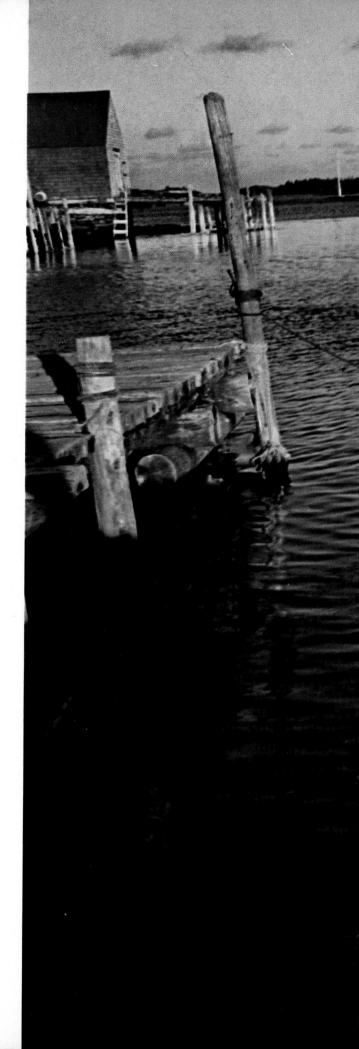

Halifax, founded by Cornwallis in 1749 as a naval
and military base against Louisbourg, is one
of the three finest natural harbours in the world.
It was the greatest convoy base in the two
World Wars of our century and before that, as a
base of the Royal Navy, it knew the
admirals from Boscawen through Nelson to Fisher.
The famous Citadel is now a museum.

Lunenburg County was settled by Protestant
Germans immediately after the founding
of Halifax. They are the oldest Canadians after
the French, but the German language
has disappeared. Old German names like Weinacht
are now spelled Whynot; Eisenhauer has
become Isnor and, by a wonderful transformation,
Bübickhöfer is now Publicover. The
Lunenburgers were the last professional seamen
under sail; Bluenose, their most famous
ship, is remembered on the Canadian ten cent piece.

RIGHT: BLUE ROCK, NEAR LUNENBURG,
      NOVA SCOTIA

BELOW: DARTMOUTH, AS SEEN FROM HALIFAX,
      NOVA SCOTIA

Louisbourg in Cape Breton
Island — once the loneliest,
foggiest, most expensively
fortified outpost of any
European power in North
America. Garrisoned by
French troops, ill-defended
by the French Navy,
unsupported by such habitant
colonists as made the defence
of Quebec an epic, Louisbourg
fell to Britain and the
New Englanders in the War
of the Austrian Succession,
was restored to France
when the war ended and was
re-fortified at such cost
that Louis XV complained
that he would soon see
the bastions of Louisbourg
rising over the horizon.
The city fell for the second
and last time in the Seven
Years' War and this opened
Wolfe's way to Quebec.
The British razed city and
fortifications to the
ground and left the site to
the fogs and seagulls.
Now the Canadian government
is rebuilding its most
impressive structures as a
national monument. These
anchors, once belonging to
eighteenth century ships
of the line, were dredged from
the bottom of Louisbourg
Harbour by the Dominion
Coal Company.

LOUISBOURG, NOVA SCOTIA

33

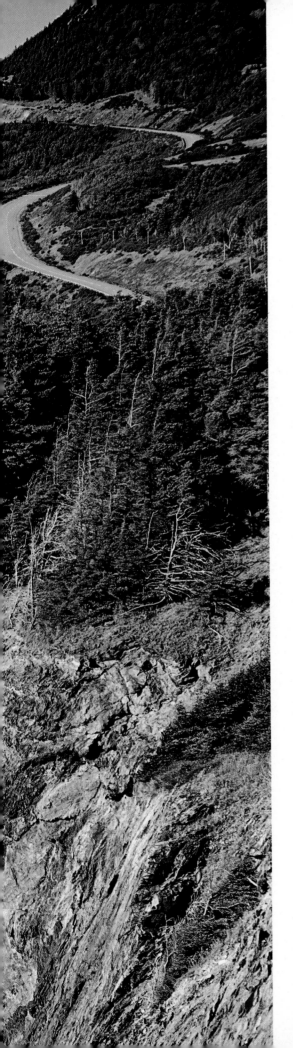

Along the Cabot Trail

No scenic highway in North America compresses into
such a short length (188 miles) such an astonishing
variety: cliffs, ocean vistas, highland glens, river
meadows and a short stretch of the Bras d'Or Lakes.
Frigid seas and grayish-pink granite on the Atlantic
shore; along the Gulf of St. Lawrence, Sienna-red cliffs
and warm water in summer, Mediterranean light on
fine days and, from Cap Rouge, a view like the one from
Taormina on the eastern coast of Sicily. The people are
mostly of Highland Scottish or French ancestry and
even now some Gaelic and French lingers.

BESIDE THE CABOT TRAIL, CAPE BRETON ISLAND, NOVA SCOTIA

Not all the Maritimes are stern and rocky; Prince Edward Island is almost a garden, famous for its potatoes, dairy products, the straightforward honesty of its people, its bathing beaches, its superb Malpeque oysters and Anne of Green Gables.

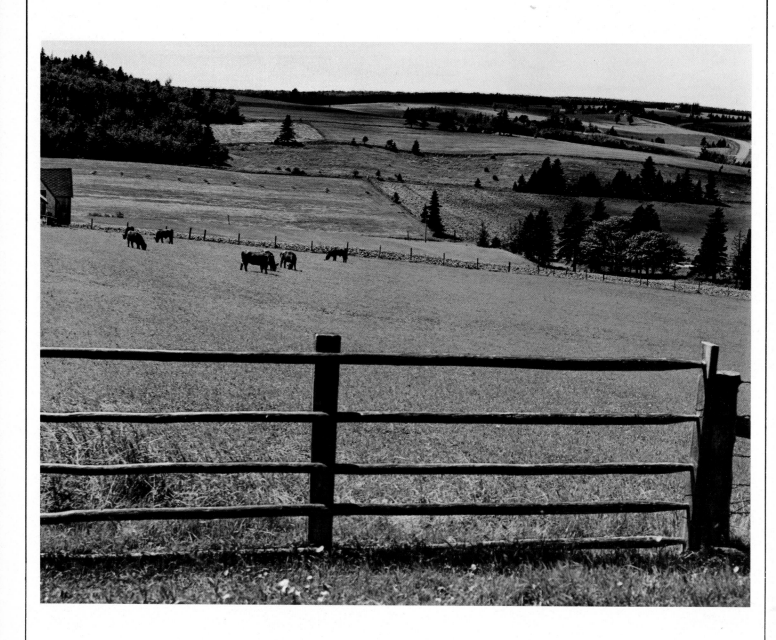

HUNTER RIVER VALLEY, PRINCE EDWARD ISLAND

The gentle island lies in the path of nor'easters from Labrador bringing blizzards in winter and drift ice in the spring which chokes the harbours. They talk hopefully of a causeway across Northumberland Strait. Will all Cape Breton Island hold enough rock for it?

SUMMERFIELD, PRINCE EDWARD ISLAND

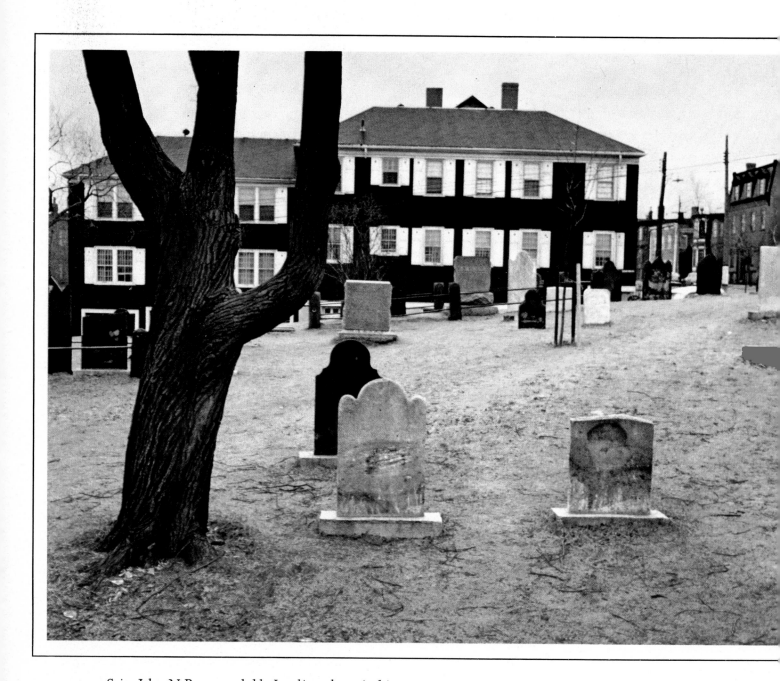

Saint John, N.B. was settled by Loyalists who arrived in
convoys in 1783; some of them were buried in this
graveyard in the city's heart. A fine harbour with a great
sea-faring tradition — here the White Star Line was
born. The Reversing Falls of the St. John River (caused
by the huge Fundy tide) divide the city from the
suburb of Lancaster. Saint John has been called the most
conservative city in Canada. It probably is.

CHURCHYARD, SAINT JOHN, NEW BRUNSWICK

A Victorian hotel of the kind that has disappeared
almost everywhere except in New Brunswick. Most
of old Loyalist Saint John perished in the fire of
1877 which gutted the city's heart. This was
the worst architectural loss in Canada's history,
for rebuilding was done in a hurry, much of
it in the red brick style of the late Victorian era.

ROYAL HOTEL, SAINT JOHN, NEW BRUNSWICK

New Brunswick is a land of rivers,
all of them beautiful and
none gigantic. Rich farms and quiet
market towns grew slowly
along the banks of the St. John,
Kennebecasis and Peticodiac and
some of the old houses are
jewels. Fredericton is surely one of
the most dignified little cities
in North America, with an
exquisite cathedral and our oldest
university. Until recently,
the St. John was the best salmon
river on the eastern side of
the continent. The dam at Beechwood,
soon to be followed by still
another dam, has reduced the salmon
somewhat, and changed the pattern
of life on the river. But great
rafts of lumber still come down from
northern New Brunswick
and northern Maine and form masses
of bobbing logs several miles
square at Maugerville. This was the
country where Sir Charles
G. D. Roberts wrote his nature
stories. In the northeast of the province
the Miramichi and the Restigouche
are famous salmon streams still.

**A RIVERSIDE HAMLET,
NEW BRUNSWICK**

The waterscapes of Nova Scotia

Bridgewater, Nova Scotia

Neil's Harbour, Nova Scotia

Pembroke, Nova Scotia

Blue Rock, Nova Scotia

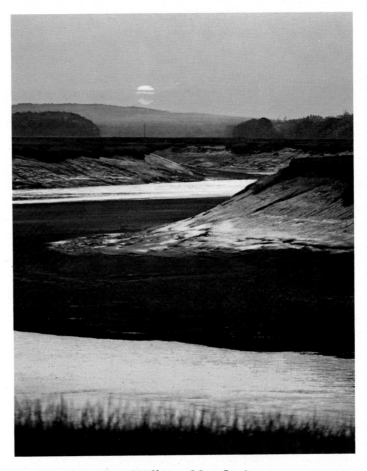

Port Williams, Nova Scotia

43

Into Quebec

When national and provincial borders were established in North America at the end of the Eighteenth Century, the decisive factor was often the movement of flowing water. Madawaska County in northern New Brunswick has a panhandle jutting into Maine because the St. John River flows into the Atlantic. The height of land between New Brunswick and Quebec is shared on the principle that such parts as drain into the Atlantic belong to New Brunswick, while those that drain into the St. Lawrence are in Quebec.

Human flows obey no such geographic laws. Northern New Brunswick is mostly French-speaking today because thousands of French Canadians seeped over the height of land to work in the forests and lumber plants of New Brunswick, or to fish the waters along the shore of the St. Lawrence Gulf. St. Leonard and Edmundston are now as "French" as La Tuque. But along the Gulf Shore, many of the French-speaking New Brunswickers are of the Acadian stock which has been there for centuries.

North-eastern New Brunswick is forest land threaded by famous rivers: the Miramichi, the Restigouche and the Matapedia which abound in salmon and feed millions of logs down to the sawmills and pulp companies at the estuaries. The Trans-Canada Highway, leaving Edmundston, mounts slowly up past Lake Temiscouta and descends the height of land to reach the St. Lawrence at Rivière du Loup, which looks across to the mountains stretching north-east from Murray Bay. The other road, paralleled by the tracks of the C.N.R., skirts Bay Chaleur with a magnificent view of the Gaspé mountains, then winds through a hundred miles of the Matapedia Valley and reaches the St. Lawrence just below Father Point, where the out-going vessels ship their pilots. Here the St. Lawrence is only nominally a river; it is really a firth of the sea—salt water deep enough to enable German submarines to operate in it during 1942, cold winds from the icebergs trapped in Belle Isle, and sometimes schools of white porpoises playing about the cutwaters of hurrying ships.

Into Quebec

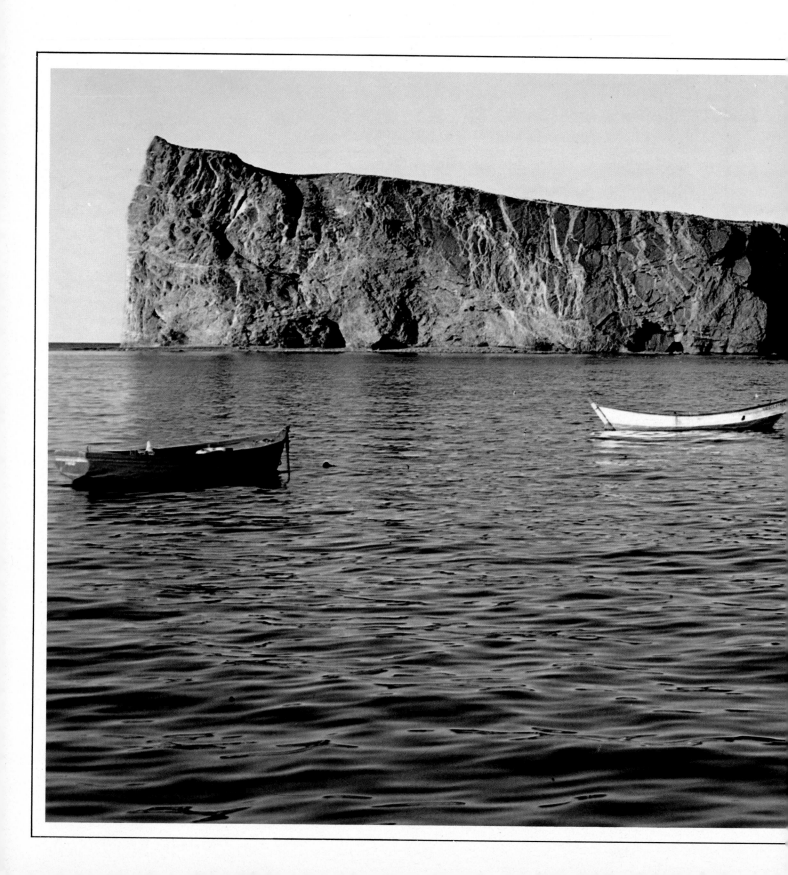

Opposite this rock Jacques Cartier is said to have landed for the first time on what now is Canadian soil and to have celebrated Mass on the beach. Percé village (behind the camera) faces it and a few miles seaward is the bird sanctuary of Bonaventure Island — a colony of gulls, gannets and puffins that dive for fish in the frigid water.

PERCÉ ROCK, QUEBEC

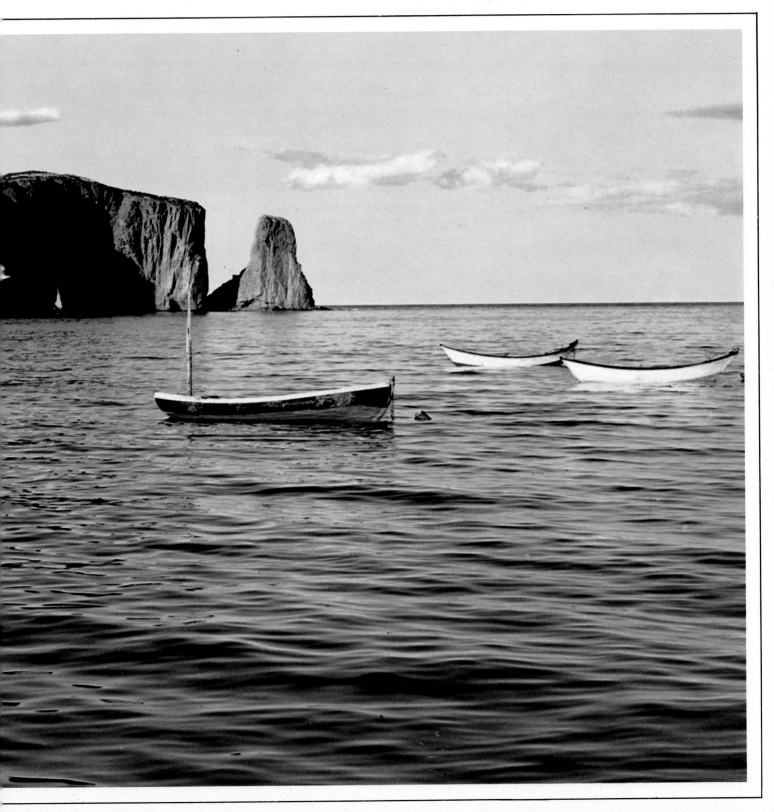

This Tadoussac church looks out on one of the world's unique spectacles — the St. Lawrence estuary, deep enough to have hidden German submarines in the war and salty enough for schools of white porpoises. What Cartier mistook for the Northwest Passage became the cradle of Canada and a water route into America's heart. Now the Seaway leads ships of the world to the Great Lake ports; also lamprey eels, which destroy the wonderful Great Lakes fish. The Seaway also tempted Montreal union leaders to make their port so costly that Halifax has gained more trade than she feared she would lose when the Seaway was originally proposed.

ALONG THE ST. LAWRENCE RIVER, TADOUSSAC, QUEBEC

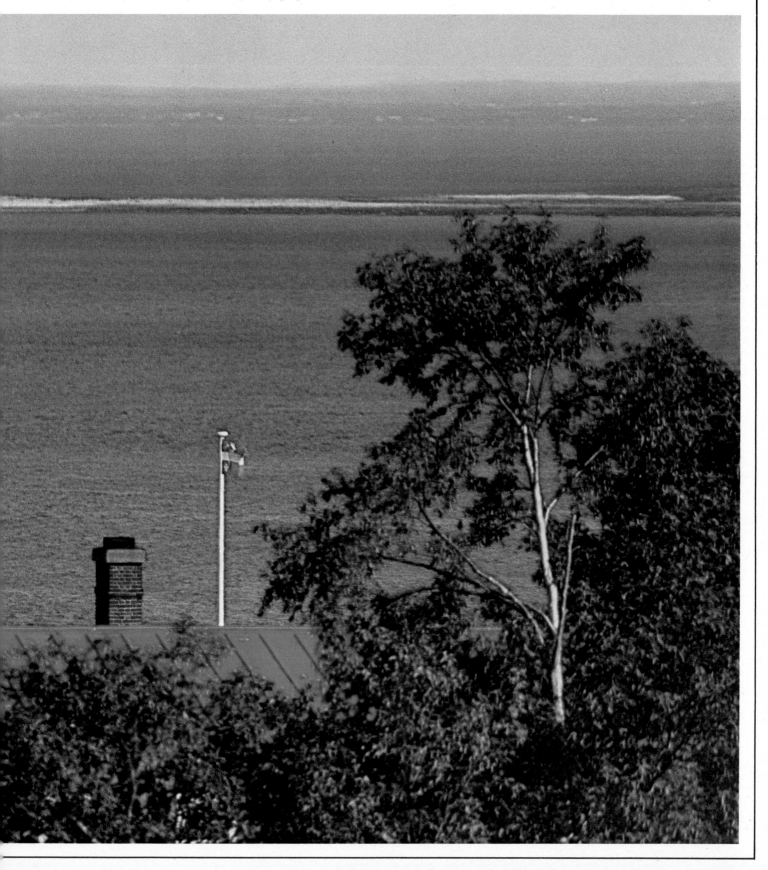

The cradle of Canada: Quebec City. Older than Boston by
some twenty-two years, Quebec has always been close to
history's heart. Champlain founded it, New France was
governed from it, epochal events have centred on men
who were associated with it: Frontenac, Laval, Montcalm,
Wolfe, Dorchester, Benedict Arnold, Nelson.
Here in 1943 Winston Churchill and Franklin Roosevelt
with their generals, admirals and airmen made the
final plans for the Normandy Invasion of June 6, 1944.

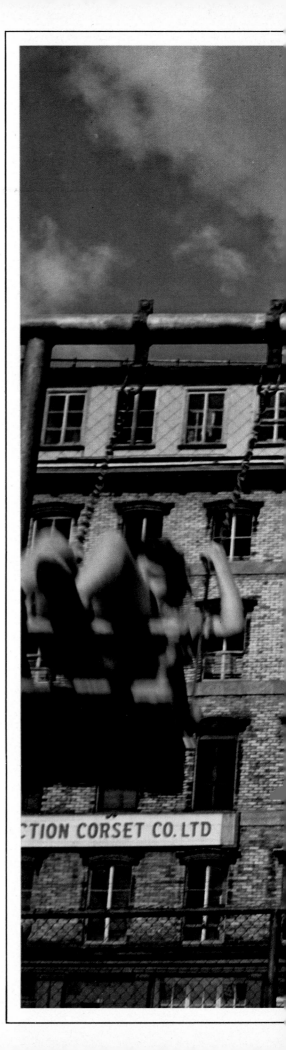

ABOVE: THE CITADEL, QUEBEC CITY;
RIGHT: LOWER TOWN, QUEBEC CITY

50

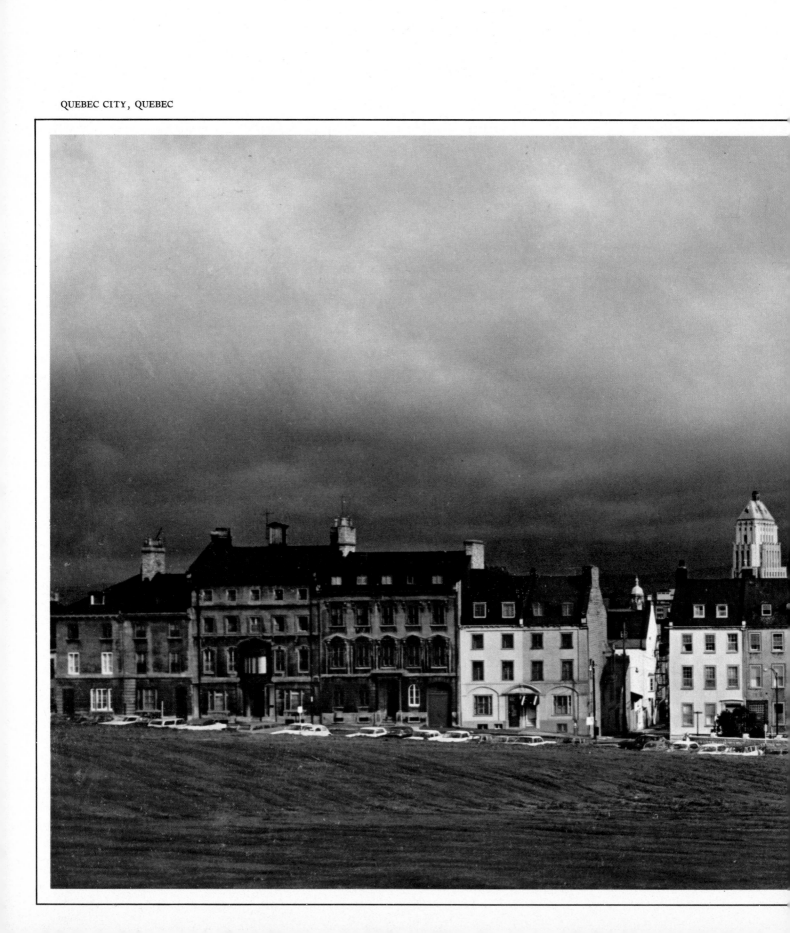

These eighteenth century French provincial houses are near the field where was fought a battle which had the most ironic results in the history of the world. It was won by the British in order to gain for their American colonists the water-entrance to the Ohio Valley. Soon afterwards, the colonists, freed at last from fear of invasion from the north, revolted against their motherland and formed the United States. The de-fenders of Quebec's Citadel repulsed the American invaders, and in 1783, when the Treaty of Versailles acknowledged the United States as an independent nation, the Union Jack flew over the Citadel the British had taken in order to incorporate the whole of North America into the British Empire. A lesson for us today, perhaps: nothing important has ever happened in Canada the way the planners and experts expected.

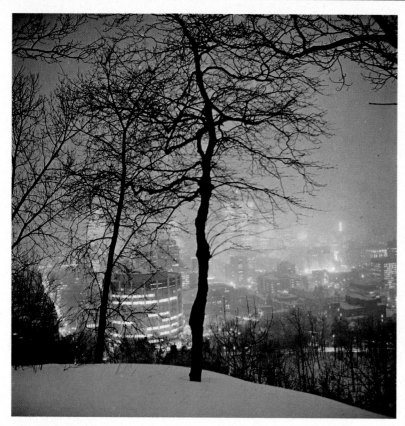

Looking down from the mountain on a hazy night transforms the functional and efficient city into a French Impressionist picture.

Montreal, French by birth but in spirit the most international city in North America. An Empire city (though without an empire) because of its location at one of the strategic points of commerce and the movements of people. Violently dramatic in climate, Montreal can be hotter than Singapore and as cold as the Arctic, as smoggy as London used to be and electrically vibrant with glittering skies when the northern weather fronts reassert themselves. Almost as criminal as Chicago, yet a city of belfries in which the angelus rings as in the Middle Ages. Half a century ago described as "an English garrison surrounded by an overgrown French village", it is now a metropolis within one step of becoming a megalopolis, a seaport with ski-slopes an hour and a half away from its skyscrapers.

THE CITY AT NIGHT, MONTREAL, QUEBEC

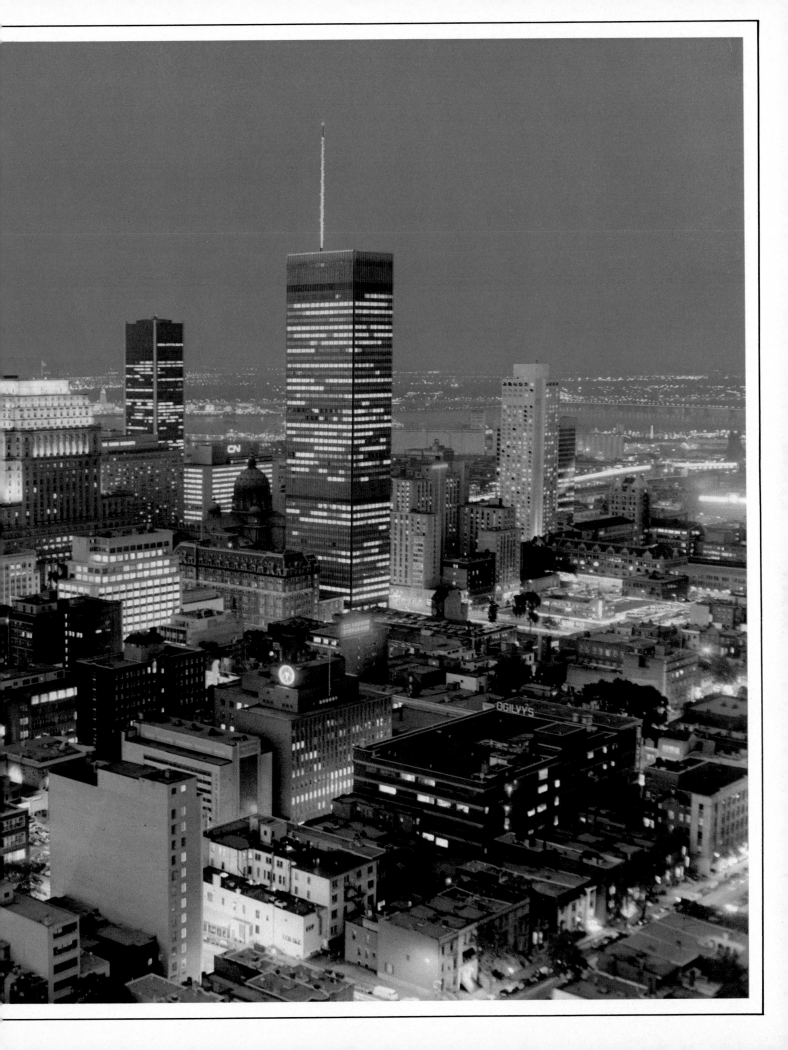

Montreal — A little old world magic in the middle of North America

Cities are like water: they seek their own
levels. If located on plains, they
spread formlessly like water in a marsh. If
constrained by nature or walls, they
concentrate their forces into a tension at
the core. Montreal lies on an island
in a river with a mountain in its centre, so
her core is concentrated.

Here are the old, the new, the powerful,
the helpless, the chic and the chi-chi,
reality and illusion for a precarious moment
linked in a bizarre harmony, ugliness
not yet triumphant, ordinariness threatening
everywhere but still held in check.

This column to Horatio Lord Nelson, situated just above Place
Jacques Cartier, is older than the one in London's Trafalgar Square.

Victorian gingerbread architecture —
fills every inch of space with porches,
railings, domes, and cupolas.

Classic transition: Upper-middle-class mansion to lower-class rooming
house to everyone's-class "maison de rendezvous" — "a boutique".

On winter evenings the cruciform forty-five storey Royal Bank Building
shines like a gigantic ice palace. Underneath it are fifty shops, eight
restaurants and one of the finest bookshops in the world; about it, the
expanse of Place Ville Marie.

A snow-covered staircase winds grace-fully downward — bearing a single set of footprints to the road below.

With its single light aglow the lamp standards illuminate the ice-covered winter scene on Mount Royal.

Twin staircases seem to lean against each other in an attitude of perfect indifference and privacy.

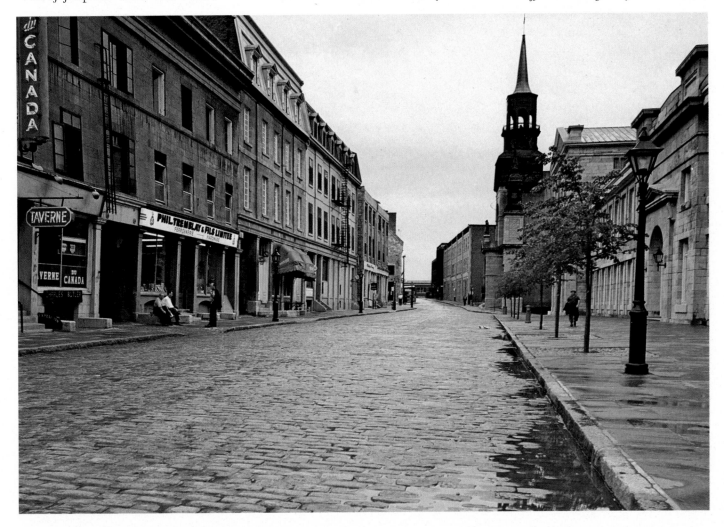

With her lamps and trees mirrored dreamily in rain water pools on worn cobblestones, the side streets of old Montreal wind down to the harbour providing a perfect contrast to the glass and steel of Place Ville Marie and the other new construction in the downtown area. The charm of eating in a three hundred year old building never fails to attract tourists.

Plunging three stories in the
concourse of Montreal's giant
Stock Exchange, a sculptured glass
chandelier sheds a new light on
the business of an old city.

PLACE VICTORIA, MONTREAL, QUEBEC

Bonsecours is the most beloved church in
Montreal. Often called the Sailors'
Chapel, it is filled for early morning
Mass by seamen, dockworkers and
the people who have brought their goods
to the nearby market. In its rear,
a statue of St. Ann with outstretched
arms blesses the harbour.

NOTRE-DAME DE BONSECOURS,
MONTREAL, QUEBEC

It has been said that Quebec's
Eastern Townships remind
everyone of some other place
they know and love. This
region was originally marked out
by Lord Dorchester as land
for Loyalists from New England.
The descendants of the old
settlers still speak in Yankee
twangs, but now the region
is predominately French-speaking
as French Canadians have
moved in from more crowded areas
to farm the land. Hence
some of the place names: Saint-
Adolfe de Dudswell, St. Paul
d'Abbotsford, Stukeley Sud and
Ham Sud. Americans have
called the Townships "a
geographical extension
of New England" – it depends upon
the point of view. There are
splendid lakes like Massawippi,
Memphramagog, Orford.
Hills like the one here, very many
of them, almost but not
quite mountains, loom over the
pasture lands and farms
and in the autumn they blaze or
glow with the scarlet of
maples, the yellow of birches,
the copper of oaks, the
pastel russet-red of butternuts.
The St. Francis is the
principal river and on its banks
is the third largest city
in Quebec. Sherbrooke, once
centred on an English
garrison (when Lord Palmerston
became Colonial Secretary
his first order was to strengthen
it against a possible
American invasion) is now largely
French-speaking.

HAM SUD,
EASTERN TOWNSHIPS, QUEBEC

60

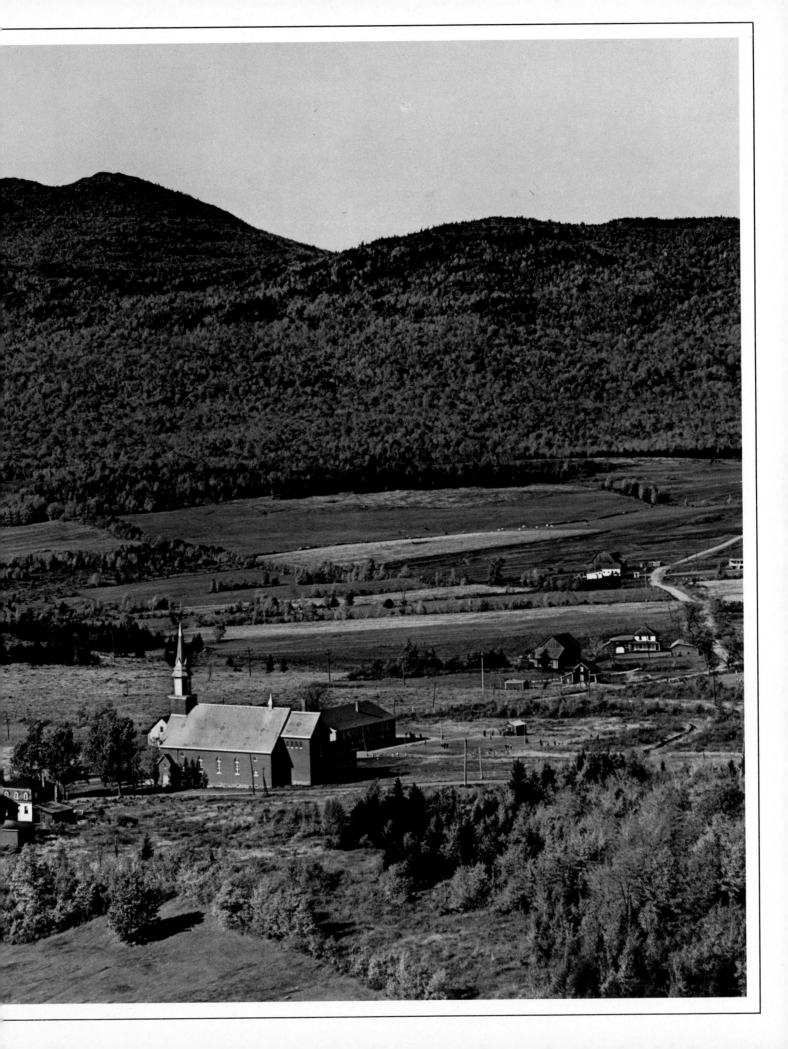

The Ottawa River, flowing from one lake into and through another, the only river in Canada whose length it is impossible to determine, the border between Quebec and Ontario, drained the Great Lakes before a geological cataclysm created the Upper St. Lawrence. A century and a half ago, it made possible the timber empire of eastern Canada.

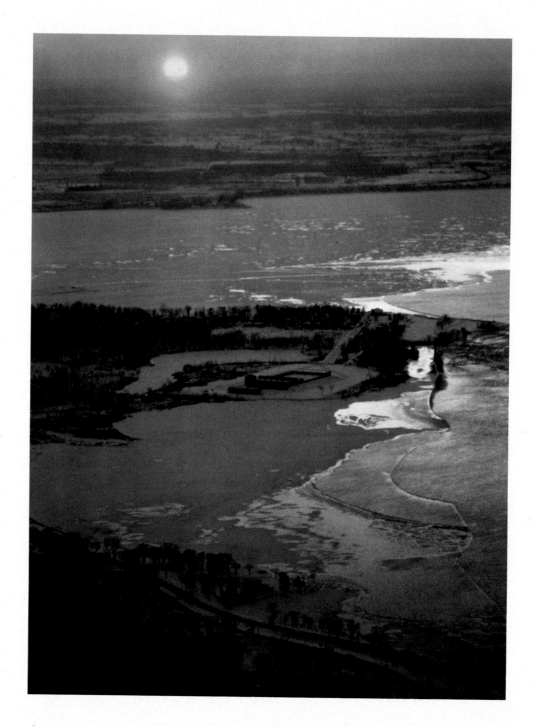

OTTAWA RIVER, THE QUEBEC-ONTARIO BOUNDARY

Up in the Laurentians

The Laurentians are best in winter,
and in Montreal "going north"
means "going ski-ing."
But before the ski-ing, French
Canadians hacked farms
out of the rare patches of arable land
in this Shield country
and built their parishes, with
simple churches like this
one in St. Faustin.

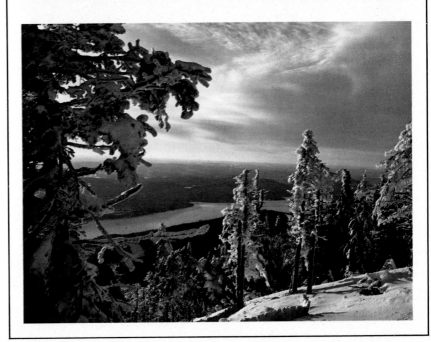

Ontario

There is no dramatic geographic division between Quebec and Ontario because both provinces are dominated by the St. Lawrence River System and the Laurentian Shield. Along and above the shores of Lakes Ontario and Erie, in the Niagara Peninsula and in the larger peninsula terminating at the Detroit and St. Clair Rivers, the Ontario land is much richer than the land in Quebec and more extensively farmed: hence the greater number of small towns and cities. But farther north the Shield country is much the same in both provinces.

The real division is ethnic and historical, Quebec having been settled by French-speaking Roman

Catholics, Ontario by Protestant Loyalists later reinforced by Protestant Scots and Irish, with the consequence that for a long time Europe's old religious rivalries continued in Canada. This particular outlet for human stupidity is now far less important than it was. "French" and "English" may still be two solitudes, but at least they are now learning to respect one another. Their joint ownership of the land makes this necessary, just as, a century ago, it made it necessary for them to form a political union. They knew that if they could not hang together, they would hang separately.

Ontario

Ottawa was the most unlikely spot anyone could imagine for a national capital. A century ago it was an over-grown lumber village noted for its drunken brawls and cholera epidemics. The decision to make it the capital of the new nation was made for the reason that most important Canadian decisions are made: no other choice seemed possible. Kingston was too close to the American border, which then was not unfortified. Montreal was too "French"; Toronto too "English". Ottawa had twin advantages: the Rideau Canal linked it to Kingston; the river to Montreal and the St. Lawrence.

Though Ottawa still has a few surviving relics of its unsightly past, some of it now is beautiful. The National Capital Commission's labours come to slow fruition in public gardens and landscaped parks. Lumbermen have given way to civil servants. The embassies of the world's nations are here. The tensions of a tense world are expressed here in the guarded understatements of men who know that lives and fortunes can hang on the words they use.

PARLIAMENT BUILDINGS,
OTTAWA, ONTARIO

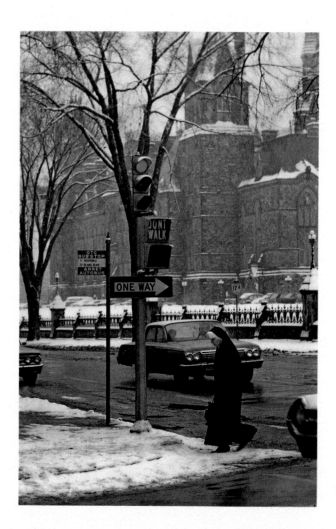

Ottawa's climate is Montreal's, only a little more so: its heat-waves in summer are breathless, its winter winds can sear the eyeballs. The city also reflects the broad linguistic divisions of the nation itself: one-third of it is French-speaking. But because its public education is still controlled by Ontario, its French-speaking citizens still must clamour for linguistic equality in their schools.

WELLINGTON STREET, OTTAWA, ONTARIO

Toronto, once the bastion of Britishdom in Canada, has suddenly become her most "ethnic" city, to the vast relief of lovers of good cooking, good music and good theatre. Canada still refrains from turning herself into an ethnic melting pot, her instinct telling her that she can survive only by encouraging human individuality.

KENSINGTON MARKET, TORONTO, ONTARIO

If a Torontonian who had died
fifteen years ago could return to life,
he could not believe this scene
at the Penny Farthing coffee house,
Yorkville. This district, a
block north of Bloor Street,
consists mainly of prettily painted
wooden houses, most of them
turned into smart boutiques and art
galleries. The espresso spots
at night are taken over by beatniks
or simply young people who
like folk-rock and yé-yé.

The great shift in Canadian
morals and mores which began
after the Hitler War is more obvious
in Toronto even than in Montreal.
The traditional puritanism has
cracked wide open — with mixed results.
The New Canadians may turn out
to be the catalytic agents who will
direct this new-found energy
into creative channels. Canada was
luckier than the United States
in the time at which she received the
human flood from the European
continent. The New Canadians who
came here after the Hitler
War, even the working classes, were
educated men and women, the
beneficiaries of the educational
reforms introduced into their native
lands in the twentieth century.

YORKVILLE AVENUE,
TORONTO, ONTARIO

The Toronto Centennial Project Ontario Place is the first
part of an entire new lakefront development programme.

ONTARIO PLACE, TORONTO, ONTARIO

OPPOSITE: CITY HALL, TORONTO, ONTARIO

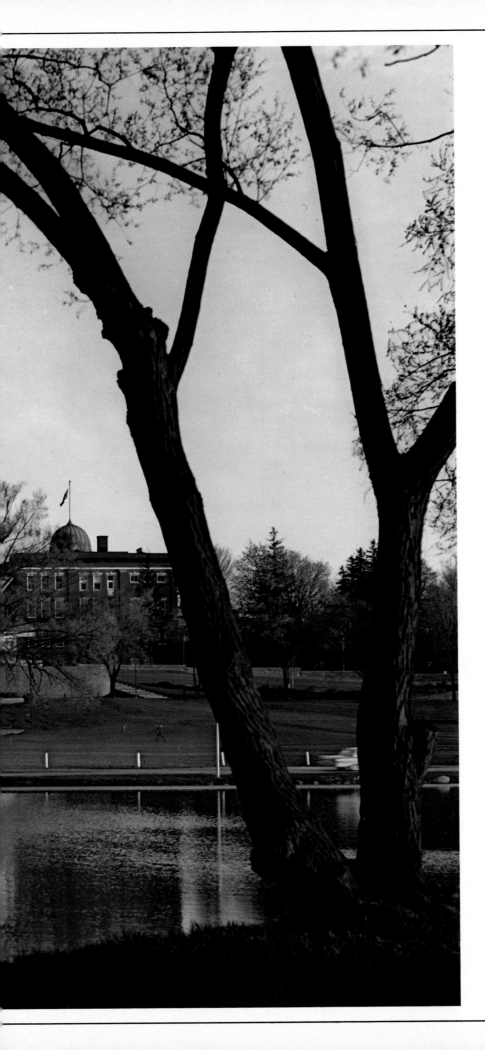

Ontarians are really the most
astonishing people in Canada.
Stratford, for years dependent on
its locomotive factories, its
most famous citizen the hockey player
Howie Morenz, as the result of a
dream in the mind of Tom Patterson,
the genius of Sir Tyrone Guthrie
and the unlocked talents of Canadian
actors from all over the country,
is now the Shakespearean centre of the
continent, with thousands of
people coming from everywhere each
summer season to see the plays
as the Elizabethans saw them. One
leaves the theatre after the
evening performance. The sky is clear,
the people move slowly, the waters
of the Avon reflect the lights:

> Look, how the floor of heaven
> Is thick inlaid with patines of
>   bright gold:
> There's not the smallest orb which
>   thou behold'st
> But in his motion like an angel
>   sings...

SHAKESPEAREAN FESTIVAL THEATRE,
STRATFORD, ONTARIO

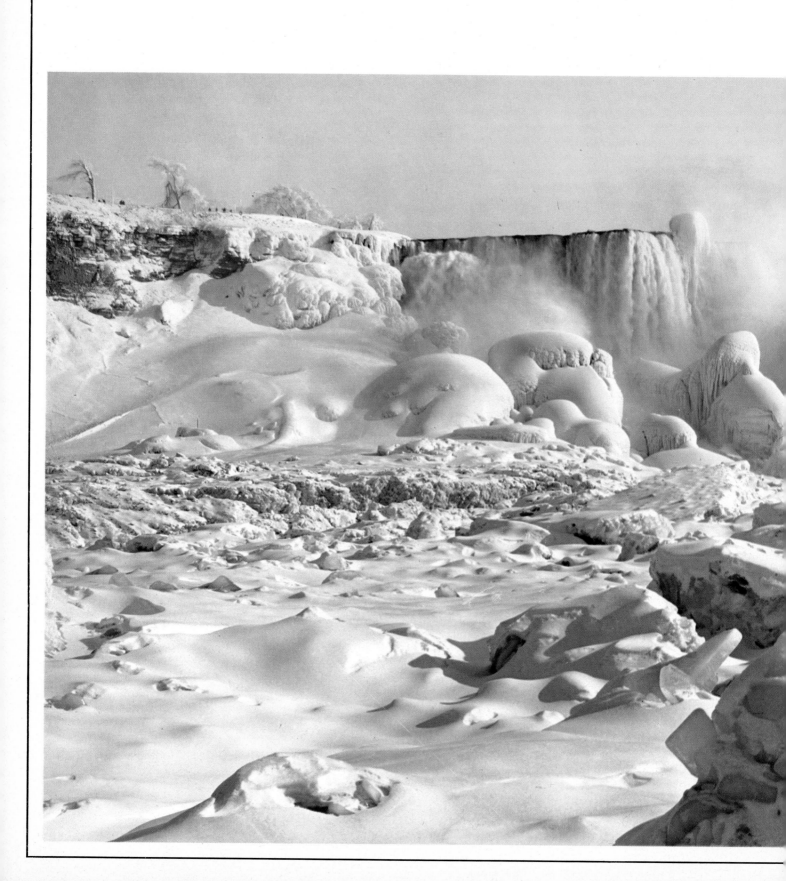

"And Niagara stuns with thundering sound"...
Goldsmith, who had never seen the Falls, imagined them
in 1770 as one of the horrors awaiting the poor folk expelled from
The Deserted Village in the time of the British enclosures.
History, the eternal ironist!

To Canadians from the Maritimes, Quebec and the Prairies, the farmland of Ontario seems almost too good to be true. It is gentle, rich and rolling, well watered, soothed by mists and moisture from the Great Lakes. In winter it seems asleep, but rarely are the winters harsh enough to kill plants. From thousands of family farms like these came the young men and women who fed the province's famous universities. Conservative as farm-bred people always are — they know that nature cannot be rushed and that forced plants are weak plants — they have always balanced the restless drive and change of Toronto, which may be the provincial capital but does not yet control the provincial legislature.

OPPOSITE: KLEINBURG, ONTARIO

The North begins in Ontario at Georgian Bay, but in summer it's warm enough for rattlesnakes. Naked rock formations stand magnificent against the sky and in the tremendous autumn storms the blowing maple leaves stain the air. It was here that Tom Thomson and his colleagues of the Group of Seven first painted the Canadian northland as it truly is, and thereby enabled millions of their countrymen to see the nature of their land.

GEORGIAN BAY, ONTARIO

The fiftieth parallel of latitude
cuts through the northern part
of Lake Nipigon in the Shield
above Lake Superior — it also
cuts through Penzance, where palm
trees flourish, through the
Somme Department of France, through
Bastôgne, Mainz and Bavaria.
In Europe these are central latitudes;
in Canada, Nipigon is part of
"the North" — spring seasons of
mosquitoes and black flies,
warm summers when the wind is south
but cold when it comes down
from the world's roof, winters colder
than in most parts of Siberia.

Here is the visible legacy of the
Great Glacier, which scraped
bare the earth's bones and gouged out
thousands of basins which now
are lakes. It will always be a
wilderness. Planes, helicopters and
bulldozers open up tiny industrial
settlements in scattered spots, but
the moment the ore-beds are
exhausted, these settlements become
ghost towns. But the North
nevertheless will make Canada
different from any other
modern nation. It is on the edge of
the settled places — the silence
of eternity always within a few hours,
or less, of a technological
civilization.

LAKE NIPIGON, ONTARIO

Vignettes of Ontario:

Patterns of leaves and trees; icicles and plenty –
Ontario's wealth is found in the city but much of
her spiritual beauty rests in the carefully tended
countryside; interchange of Highways 400 and 401,
Toronto – Scarborough Bluffs, near Toronto.

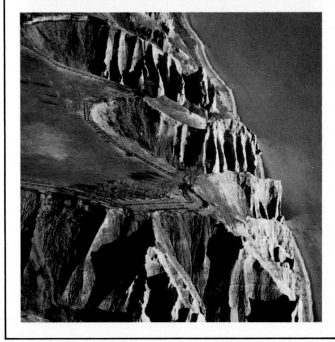

Across the Prairies

From Ottawa to the Prairies along the line of the Canadian Pacific you travel for a night, a day and most of the night following and nearly all of this journey is through the empty land of the Shield, the train wiggling like a mechanical snake around little lakes, with aspens and spruce blurring past the windows. Before sunset in summer you reach Lake Superior and it is like coming upon an ocean. Port Arthur and Fort William . . . then into the Shield again and at dawn you are at Kenora and the Lake-of-the-Woods. Living in a few hours through that appalling terrain, you may think back and try to imagine the miracle of the voyageurs who reached

Fort William, birchbark canoes, four tons of trade-goods and 36 portages, in thirty-six to forty days.

Then the rocks thin out. Suddenly you see black earth appearing and then you are in a land-ocean, the black prairie of Manitoba, on the horizon is a grain elevator and the onion dome of a Ukrainian church.

The breaching of the frontier between Ontario and the West is still the greatest achievement in the history of Canada. In this age of masses and abstractions, let it not be forgotten that this was the work of a very few men, that guts and imagination working together are the expression of the Divine in human life.

The Prairies

Not so long ago – perhaps no longer
ago than 15,000 years –
the eastern Canadian prairie lay
under the waters of Lake Agassiz,
which rapidly drained off
into Hudson Bay as the Ice Cap
receded. When the lake still
covered the land, it drained off
through the Great Lakes
and the St. Lawrence. Lake of the
Woods, the Red River and the
prairie lakes – Winnipeg, Winnipegosis,
Manitoba – are its survivals.
So is the black earth of Manitoba,
enriched by thousands of years
of dead and decayed marine life. So,
for that matter, is the
tableflat land itself, crushed by
quadrillions of tons of ice.

A land – sea, flat in Manitoba,
rolling a little in Saskatchewan,
and above it prairie skies
like the one in this picture. Often
when you drive along a prairie
road like this, running straight to
the horizon, you have the illusion
that something is the matter
with your car – that it has become
stationary. When you fly
across it after dark it seems to be
dotted with fireflies –
lights from barns and the windows
of farmhouses, with occasionally
a blaze of light that is a city
or town. This is a land that can best
be described in music, but
the music to describe it has yet
to be written.

THE QUEEN'S HIGHWAY,
SASKATCHEWAN

86

Wheat for the world, including Russia and China.
From the air, especially in spring, much of the Saskatchewan
prairie resembles a modern art gallery, the rectangular
sectional farms with their curving tree-lines, planted against
erosion, forming the designs, the blue-green of
young wheat contrasting with the dark earth of ploughed land.

HARVEST PATTERNS, SASKATCHEWAN

AN ISLAND OF ELEVATORS IN A SEA OF GRAIN

The towns with their grain elevators are like ships
in this land-sea. Also, just as at sea, the weather dominates.
The movement of clouds, their rapid changes of colour,
make the wind visible. When the wheat is ripe, it writhes in
the wind, it boils in the wind, ominously gold under the
darkened sky, Van Gogh's wheatfield near Arles on a colossal scale.

STORM THREATENING OVER THE WHEATLANDS

91

Who Has Seen The Wind—
*the verb is the decisive word in
the title of W. O. Mitchell's
wonderful novel of a boy
growing up on the prairie, discovering
life, love, cruelty, fear
and God in the movement of grain,
in the sound of the wind,
in the prairie birds and animals.
A land which might have produced
Hebraic prophets looking up
to that appalling sky and asking
the Creator, "What is man,
that thou art mindful of him" and
more than once coming to the
conclusion that He is not. Mitchell's
phrase that here life is reduced
to "the common denominator of sky and
Saskatchewan prairie" serves
better than reams of analysis to
explain the feeling of prairie
people that their life is unique,
that the people in the East
and on the Pacific Coast can never
really understand them.
It explains the almost perpetual
political opposition of the
prairie provinces to whatever is the
ruling party in the central
Canadian government.*

ABOVE: STORM SKY, THE PRAIRIES;

RIGHT: WHEAT AT HARVEST

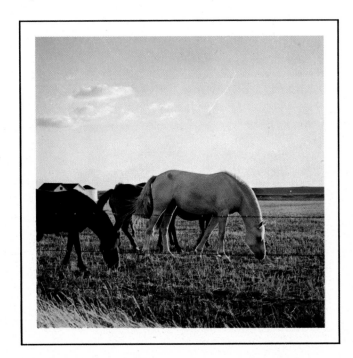

Bleak — yes. Yet, so mysterious is beauty, haunting.
The stark word PIONEER is still apt
on this grain elevator on a siding of the trans-
continental railway line which links it to
Montreal and Vancouver. On these plains when
the first settlers came in, the creak of
the wooden wheels in the Red River carts sounded
for miles; then came the lonely wail of the
whistles on the steam locomotives; now, there's the
penetrating blare of the new horns on the Diesels.

ABOVE: HORSES GRAZE THE WESTERN PASTURE

LEFT: TRACKSIDE GRAIN ELEVATORS

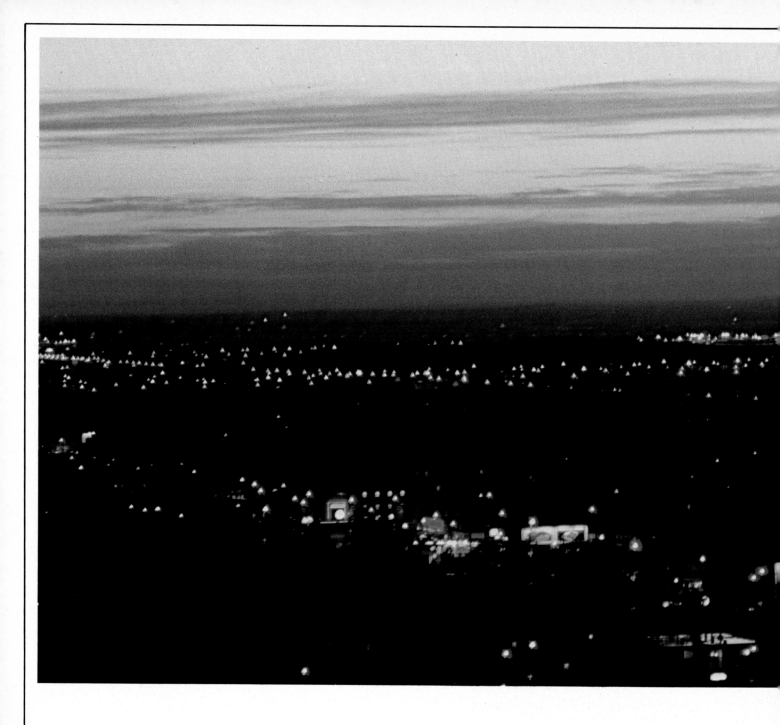

Prairie cities — here Edmonton, Winnipeg and Calgary where the land is flat and where the winter temperature is often fifty below zero, the people stay mostly indoors though they have come to work in their cars. The people — it is in the cities, when you reach them across the plains, that you begin to grasp what they have done in such a little time. Apart from the Red River Settlement, out of which Fort Garry grew into Winnipeg, all the development on the Prairies post-dates Confederation. The inarticulate courage of the pioneers can scarcely be reached with the imagination. They came out with their families on the colonist cars — came out to a land without trees, and therefore without wood to build shelters. Thousands of them began their lives in sod huts just as the Russians did long ago in the steppes. But look at the cities now! When the oil came in, some of them possibly got rich too quick. But their universities, a generation ago lacking in nearly everything, now teem with students, and some of the best scientists in the land are in their staffs.

WINNIPEG — GATEWAY TO THE WEST AND CANADA'S FOURTH LARGEST CITY.

THE IMPRESSIVE ARCHITECTURE OF EDMONTON'S PARLIAMENT BUILDINGS.

MODERN SCULPTURE, CALGARY

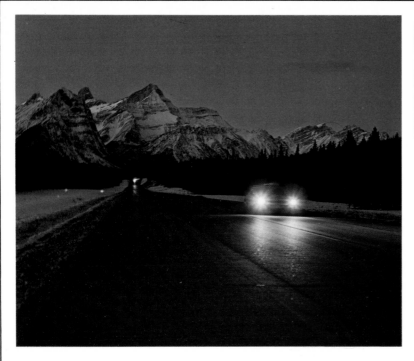

Banff National Park preserves 2,564 square miles of breathtaking scenery and is the oldest and most popular of Canada's national parks. Jasper National Park, one of the largest parks on the continent, extends along the eastern slope of the Canadian Rockies in the western part of Alberta, with Banff National Park joining its boundary to the south and Mount Robson Provincial Park in British Columbia adjoining it to the west.

ABOVE: HIGHWAY THROUGH THE ROCKIES

OPPOSITE: SKIING IN THE ROCKIES

BELOW: BETWEEN BANFF AND JASPER NATIONAL PARKS

When you travel across the far western prairie the dramatic moment
comes, not when you see the skyline of the Rockies, but
when you reach the visible tilt where the prairie begins to rise.
This moment does not come until you have passed the
110th parallel of longitude – farther south, in Colorado, the
moment arrives some eight parallels of longitude farther east,
the Canadian prairie being wider than the American because the
Rockies swerve easterly south of the border. At Calgary
the foothills begin, rolling like the smaller waves that herald
the moment of the titanic seas of a hurricane.
Beyond them the earth-waves are grey, minaretted, the earth
in tempest all the way to the Pacific.

WILD FLOWERS IN THE ALBERTAN FOOTHILLS

British Columbia

The natural division between the Prairies and the cordilleran West is the most dramatic of them all. The Great Divide in the so-called Canadian Rockies marks the line of demarcation between Alberta and British Columbia. This is the range of mountains which separates the waters flowing easterly to reach the Atlantic through Hudson Bay, and westerly to reach the Pacific. In the case of the Peace and Athabasca rivers, the waters drain through the Mackenzie Basin to the Artic. The Columbia Icefield, straddling the Divide, is the source of major rivers which reach all three oceans.

The piercing of the vast ranges of the British Columbia mountains by the railways was Canada's greatest single response to the physical challenge of her environment. The success of Confederation depended upon it. In our time, the bulldozer has

enabled the magnificently scenic Trans-Canada
Highway to make it possible for automobiles to pass
through the ranges on comfortable grades all the
way to the coast.

Among the wisest acts ever performed by federal
parliament were the ones which created the national
parks—Waterton Lakes (which is part of the
International Peace Park straddling the U.S. border),
Banff, Yoho, Jasper, Kootenay and others. Though
Banff and Jasper are technically in Alberta, they
belong to the cordilleran region of the Canadian West.
Here, if nowhere else on this progressive continent,
the balance of nature still holds. Elk, moose,
deer, antelope, bears black and grizzly, marmots,
and other rodents, even wolves, live without
fear of the hunter and anyone can see them
who visits the parks.

British Columbia

INLAND PASSAGE, CALVERT ISLAND, BRITISH COLUMBIA

The British Columbia coast from the border north to the Alaskan Panhandle is about 550 miles. Yet the actual coastline in that maze of twisting fiords and islands is estimated to be more than 16,000 miles — five times as long as Canada is wide. The greatest weight of living matter per acre in the world is found in areas such as Vancouver Island's Cathedral Grove, where there are still virgin stands of the coastal rain forest's tremendous Douglas firs, cedars, hemlocks and Sitka spruce. North America's highest peaks are found in the Coast Mountain System and its Alaskan extension. Mount McKinley, at 20,300 feet is the continent's highest. Mount Logan, 19,850 feet, Canada's highest, is in the St. Elias Mountains of southwestern Yukon.

British Columbia's rivers are the most spectacular
on the continent. The incredible Fraser, charging down
the Rocky Mountain Trench, bending around
the Cariboo, confined in its canyon all the way down
to Hope, passing tranquilly through the nation's
most beautiful farmed valley into its delta, issuing in
the Georgia Strait, is as long as the Rhine and is
the greatest salmon breeder in the world. Here we see
the Thompson, named after the geographer of
the North West Company. At Lytton it smashes into the Fraser
like a liquid battering ram, blue water sharp
against the Fraser's brown, then is swallowed and disappears.

THOMPSON RIVER, BRITISH COLUMBIA

The Kootenay, four hundred miles long,
rises in the B.C. Rockies, flows south into Montana and
Idaho, then bends north and returns to Canada
to enter Kootenay Lake, a lake seventy-five miles long,
so magnificent that the only word fit to describe
it is its own name. Leaving the lake, it discharges into
the Columbia, which flows south across the American border.
The character of these mountain rivers is schizophrenic:
where the drop is rapid and they are confined, they are raging
torrents of incalculable power; wherever the flow slackens, they
are tranquil vistas of water reflecting the sky.

KOOTENAY RIVER, BRITISH COLUMBIA

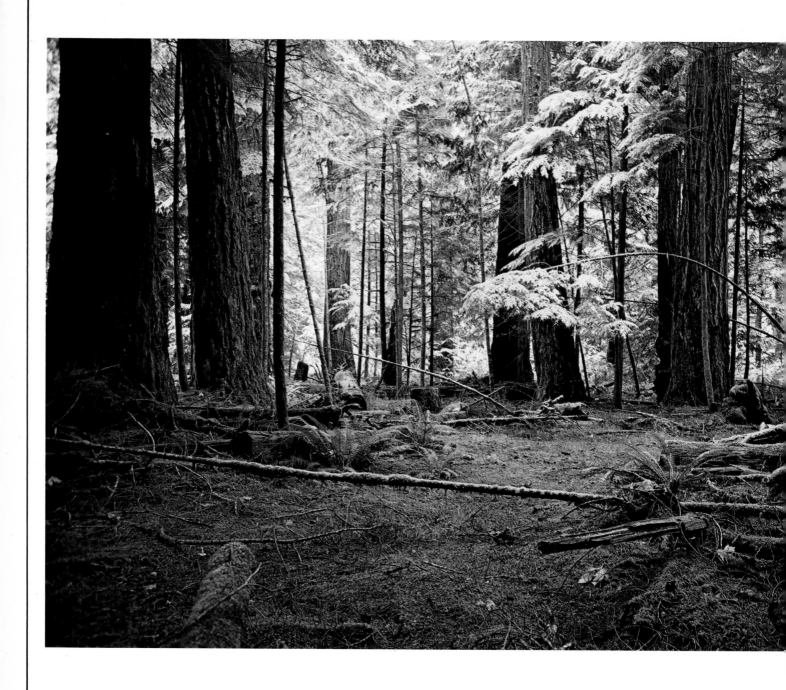

ABOVE: RAIN FOREST, VANCOUVER ISLAND

OPPOSITE: TOTEM POLES AT STANLEY PARK, VANCOUVER ISLAND

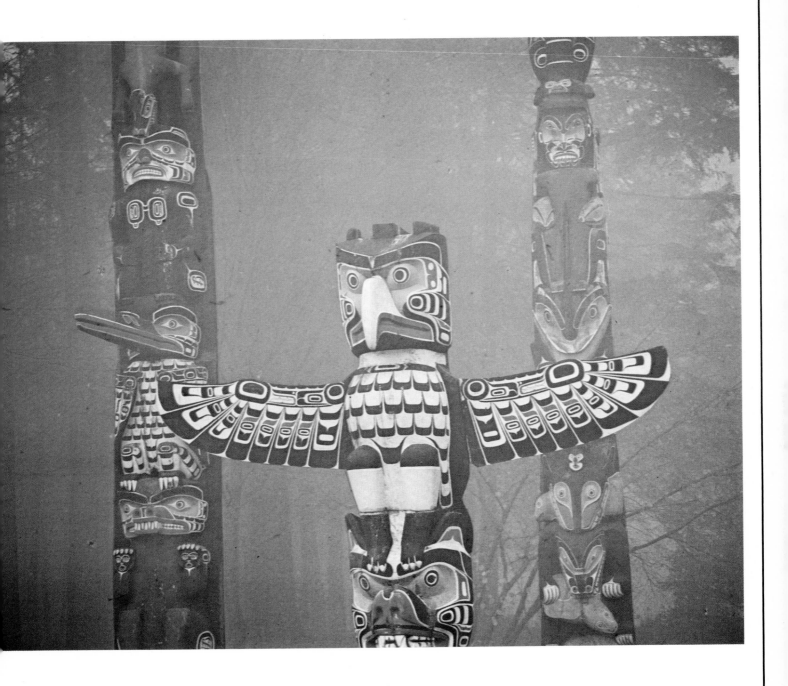

Civilization in its early stages resulted from inertia: the invention of agriculture stopped nomadic habits and pinned the people long enough in one place to enable them to foster crafts and arts. On the British Columbia coast the abundance of salmon played this role. It held the people to the river mouths. When Alexander Mackenzie encountered the Indians of the coast he marvelled at their art, but even more did he marvel at their skill with canoes. He said they were superior to his own voyageurs, the ultimate accolade.

The Douglas firs of British Columbia, some of them, are more than a thousand years old. In the Redpath Museum of McGill University is a cross section of one of them, its inner rings indicating its age. When it first began to grow, Alfred the Great was King of England.

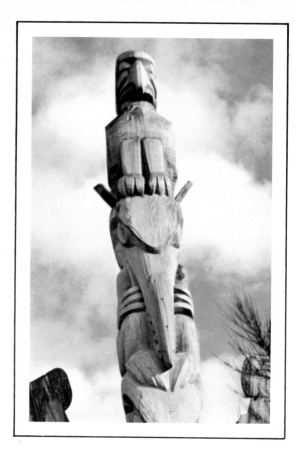

Among some primitive cultures (not confined
to the New World by any means) the individual
human being was supposed to have a mystical,
or even a real, relationship to some animal,
plant, bird or inanimate object. Whatever this
was became his totem. The man might be
a descendant of his totem, or the two might be
descended from a common ancestor. The man
might be prohibited from killing or eating the
animal, bird or plant that is his totem.
A group or a tribe, or parts of different tribes,
might have the same totem and be prohibited
from marriage within the totem kin. Nowhere have
such magnificent specimens of totem art
survived as in the coast of British Columbia.
The genius of the painter Emily Carr
has distilled the essence and beauty of them,
together with their mysterious meaning.

ABOVE: TOTEM POLES AT ALERT BAY,
        BRITISH COLUMBIA

RIGHT: A FALLEN TOTEM AT KISPIOX,
        BRITISH COLUMBIA

Vancouver, the western terminus of
the railway lines that made
Canada a nation, on the sheltered
waters of the Georgia Strait,
its site discovered in the
eighteenth century by the British
naval explorer Captain George
Vancouver, has the most enviable
future of any city in Canada.
It has grown with astonishing
speed from a small lumber
town into Canada's third-largest
city. The measure of its
growth, in terms of time, can be seen
in the University of British
Columbia situated on a peninsula
jutting out into the Strait.
As late as 1917, this was still
a branch of McGill's Extension
Department; now it is the second-
largest university in
the land, and still growing.

The buildings in this picture
are brand-new. Here is the
esthetically justifiable use of
the high-rise, at least for
the tenants with a seaward view.
When one comes to Vancouver
and looks around, one feels like
saying a prayer to its citizens:
"You can make this city a
western Athens if you wish it to
become immortal, and not a bonanza
for real estate speculation.
Please, please do it!"

HIGH-RISE APARTMENTS,
VANCOUVER,
BRITISH COLUMBIA

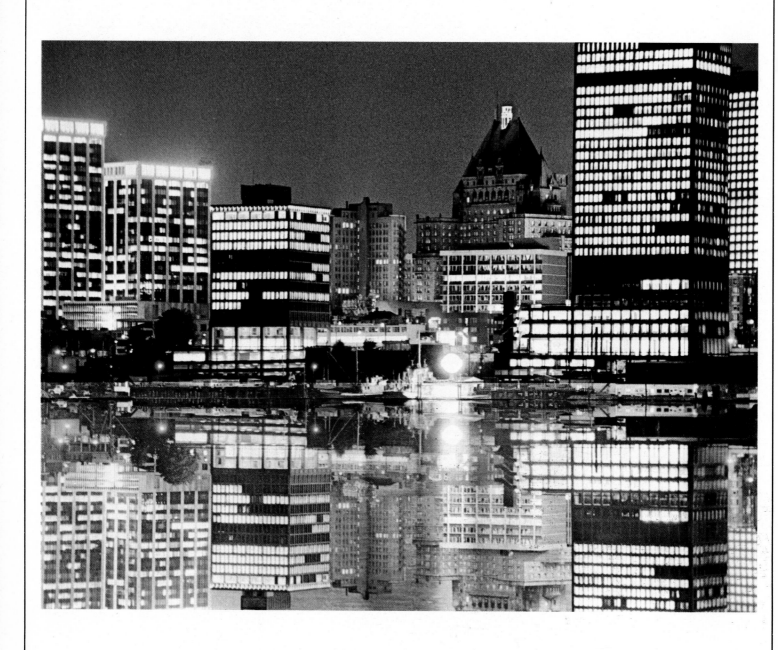

Here the engineers and planners have not failed. The Lions Gate Bridge perfectly combines utility with art, which always conspires with nature. At night, in fog, or in sun, this bridge never lets its setting down. It never seeks to impose itself upon its surroundings. It becomes part of them, and by so doing, helps to define them.

LIONS GATE BRIDGE, VANCOUVER, BRITISH COLUMBIA

OPPOSITE: LIGHTS OF VANCOUVER'S WATERFRONT
ARE REFLECTED IN BURRARD INLET

Stanley Park has an aquarium, a small zoo
with native animals and reptiles, gardens,
flowering shrubs and giant trees. Salt water
laps its shores; in fog it is mysterious;
in fine weather the sun filters through the
branches as in this picture. But its mood is
natural, and what men have done to improve
it does not obtrude on its wonderful natural
setting. It is a pleasant thought that
the seaward tip of Canada's Atlantic port,
Halifax, is also a natural park, though
there the trees are nearly all spruce and pines,
and in winter it is cold. It never seems
cold in Stanley Park. The air is soft as it
is in Cornwall and the climate much the same.

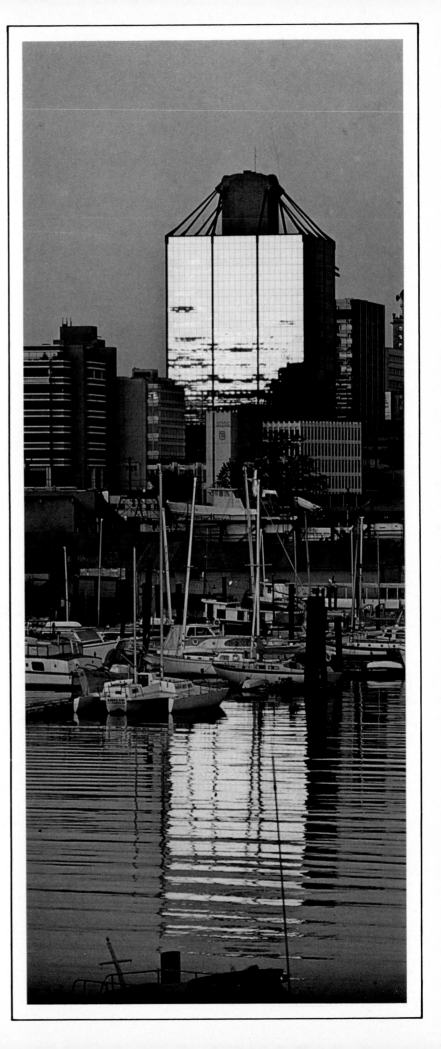

LEFT: STANLEY PARK,
VANCOUVER, BRITISH COLUMBIA

RIGHT: VANCOUVER'S MODERN
SKYLINE, SEEN FROM THE HARBOUR

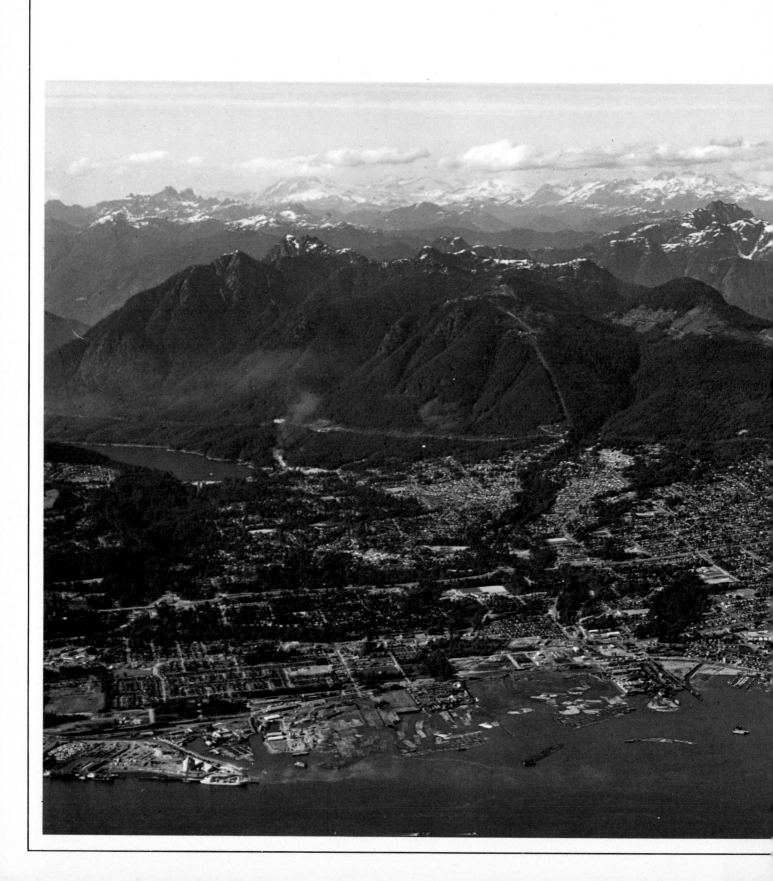

North Vancouver photographed from an aircraft at
nine thousand feet: the Coast Mountains dusted with snow;
Lynn and Seymour Canyons striking up through
the ranges on the right; left-centre, the line of the chair
lift going up the side of Grouse Mountain;
in the docks, ships bound for any port on the Pacific.

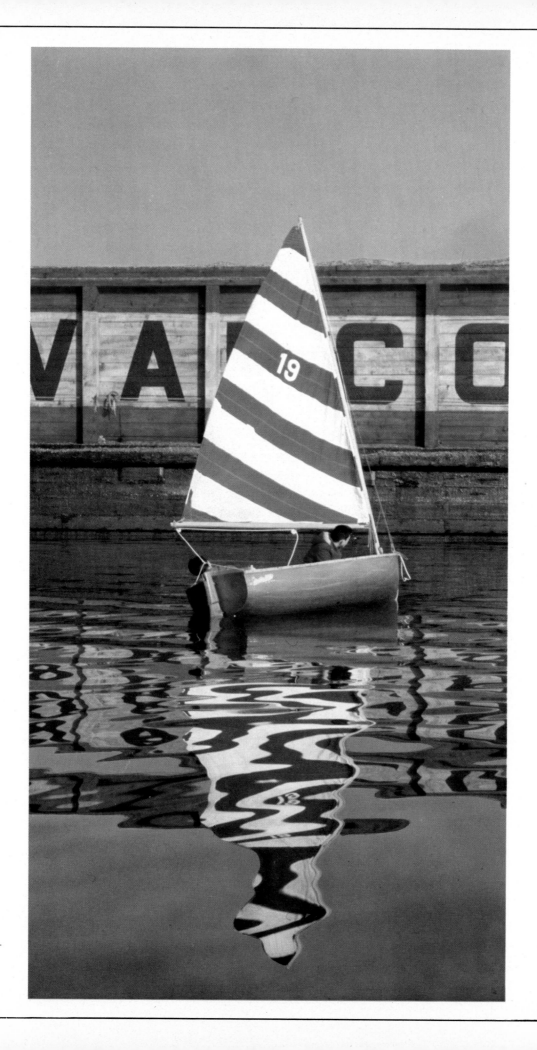

The sheltered waters of Georgia Strait, with Vancouver Island acting as a gigantic breakwater against the ocean surges, is almost perfect for yachting and small-boat cruising. In the outer harbour small boys can learn to sail in dinghies. Larger craft have the prospect of the whole British Columbia coast.

YACHT CLUB, WEST VANCOUVER, BRITISH COLUMBIA

OPPOSITE: IN VANCOUVER HARBOUR, BRITISH COLUMBIA

The spectacular indentations of the coastline about Vancouver spare the citizens from the curious melancholy that affects people (whether they know it or not) who live facing an uninterrupted horizon on a western ocean—the sight of the setting sun being swallowed in the sea as though it had perished out of the world. Here the setting sun haloes promotories and islands.

Vancouver Island—285 miles long, in places 3,000 feet high, coastline indented by deep inlets; moist Pacific winds; unspoiled streams plentiful in salmon and steelhead; small lakes in the interior; orchards, farms, lumber mills and beaches.

ABOVE: SEASCAPE, VANCOUVER, BRITISH COLUMBIA

RIGHT: ON LONG BEACH, VANCOUVER ISLAND, BRITISH COLUMBIA

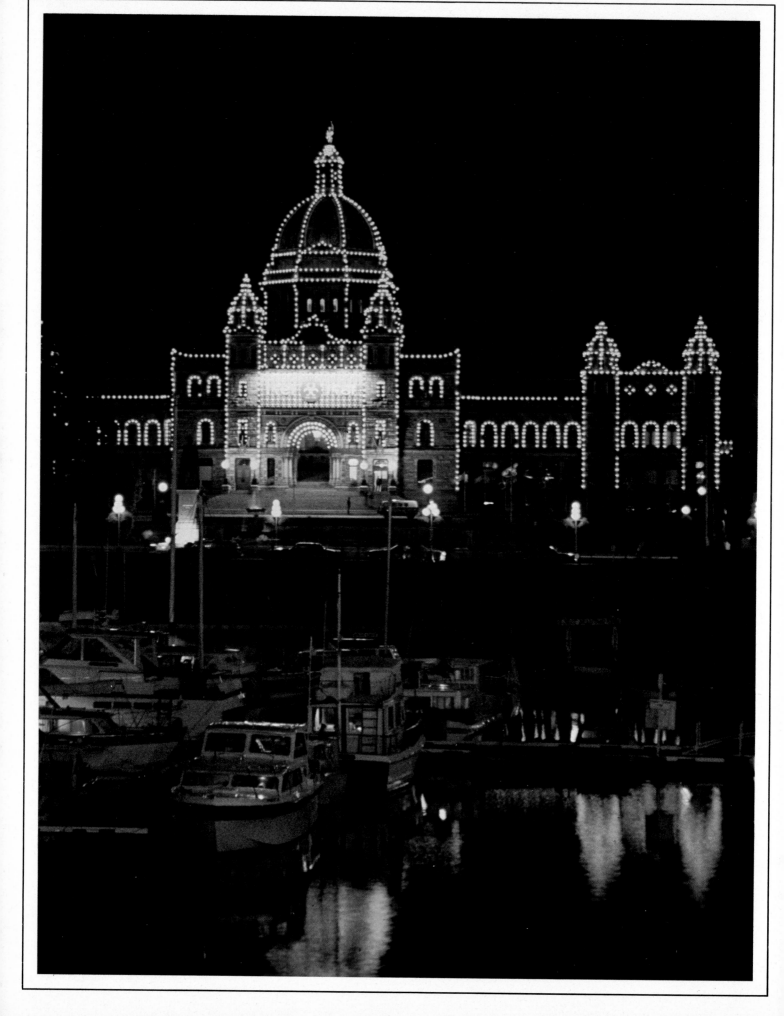

Victoria, capital of British
Columbia, was founded in
1843 as a Hudson's Bay Company's
trading post known as
Fort Camosun, later renamed
Victoria in honour of
the Queen. Its suburb, Esquimalt,
is the eastern base of the
Canadian Navy. It became the capital
of the province in 1866,
is the western base of the
Confederation and five years before
British Columbia joined Canada
as the sixth province (one year after
Manitoba). When we remember
that, in 1870, Victoria was divided
from "Canada" by more than
two thousand miles of Shield country,
prairies almost empty of
humanity, by hundreds of miles of
mountains, the boldness of
this decision takes the breath away.
As a Canadian newspaper
recently pointed out, if computers had
existed a century ago such a decision
would never have been made.
All the evidence that men could
have fed into it would have
said "no" to it . . .

OPPOSITE:
PARLIAMENT BUILDINGS,
VICTORIA, BRITISH COLUMBIA

RIGHT:
THE WESTERN OCEAN,
FROM VANCOUVER ISLAND,
BRITISH COLUMBIA

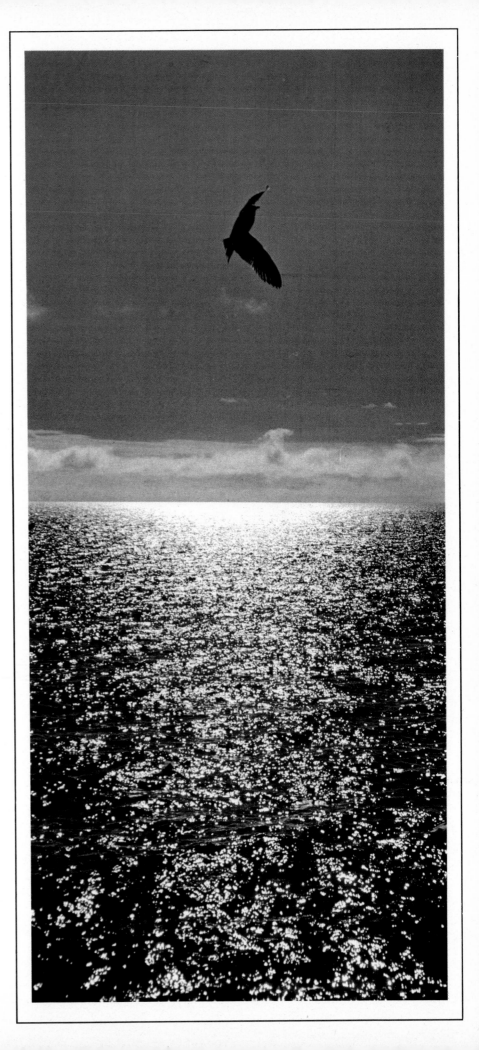

The journey ends

The cameras have come to the end of a
journey which began in Newfoundland
and ended in Vancouver Island. They
have tried to follow the long thread of
settlement from coast to coast. They
have omitted most of Canada; how
could they possibly have included more
than a minuscule suggestion of the
enormous land?

We live in a world so filled by the
inspirational messages of professional
phrase-makers, commercial and political,
that we have bred a generation whose
ears are sealed to the truth even if the
truth is optimistic. We live in a world
so stupefied and confused by scientific
surveys, opinion polls, computerized
predictions that most of us for the sake
of our sanity make our separate peace-
pacts with these insensate abstractions. In
Canada we are still asking ourselves the
question, "Who are we?" It would be
better to look at what we are and what
the nation has done in so short a time.

In the Funeral Oration delivered by
Pericles to the Athenians more than
four hundred years before Christ, he
made the classic understatement: "Our
city is superior to the report of her."

Canada would not look like much if she
were merely superior to the report of her
given by a lot of her citizens. The fact
is that her record is almost incredible.
Now after a long winter of subter-
ranean growth, her artists and writers,
musicians and dancers are beginning to
express her meaning not only to their
own people but to the outside world.
She is joining articulate civilization
and is earning her right to do so.

Hugh MacLennan

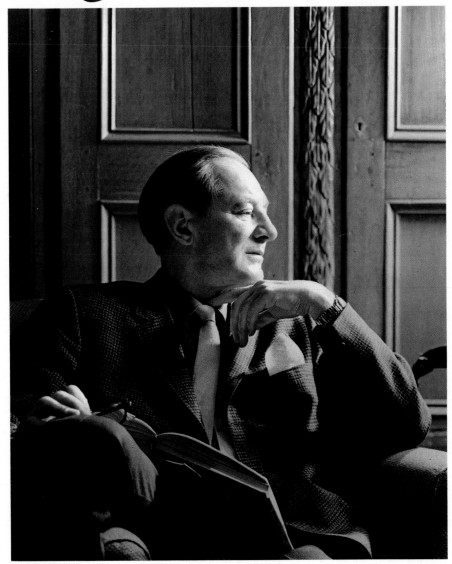

The author of the text of this book is one of Canada's most distinguished novelists. Born in Nova Scotia, he won a Rhodes scholarship and studied at Oxford and, later, at Princeton. He is now at McGill University with the rank of Professor of English, a subject he never studied formally. His great contribution to Canadian literature has been recognized by the conferment of honorary degrees and he has been translated into many languages. A fellow of the Royal Society of Canada and of the Royal Society of Literature (London), he has been given Governor-General's awards for his novels Two Solitudes, The Precipice and The Watch That Ends The Night, and for two volumes of essays. In 1967 he was made a Companion of the Order of Canada. He is still writing.

Picture Credits

Order of appearance in the text
of pictures listed here
is left to right, top to bottom,
After the first recording,
principal sources are credited
under these abbreviations:

PB   Paul Baich
RB   Roloff Beny
BB   Bob Brooks
BD   Barbara Deans
JDV   John de Visser
MD   Mike Dobel
HE   Horst Ericht
GH   George Hunter
JL   Jack Long
M   Malak
MS   Miller Services
DN   Don Newlands
EEO   Eberhard E. Otto
PT   Peter Tasker
PV   Peter Varley
DW   Doug Wilkinson

COVER   George Hunter
1   GH
2   Peter Tasker
4   Doug Wilkinson;
Roloff Beny; GH
5   Eberhard E. Otto
(from Miller
Services);
Malak; Jack Long

13   DW
14   DW
16   GH
18-19   Fred Bruemmer
20-21   DW
22   RB
23   RB
24-25   M (from MS)
26   John de Visser
27   JDV
28   EEO (from MS)
29   RB
30   Horst Ericht
31   Peter Varley
32-33   RB
34-35   EEO (from MS)
36   M (from MS)
37   Bob Brooks
38   HE
39   HE
40-41   M (from MS)
42   BB
43   BB; BB; BB; BB
46-47   EEO (from MS)
48-49   Barbara Deans
50   JDV
51   JDV
52-53   Rene Delbuguet
54   Paul Baich
55   Henry Koro
56   JDV; Sam Tata;
JDV; JDV

57   BD; BD; BD;
Canadian National
Railway
58   JDV
59   JDV
60-61   GH
62   RB
63   M (from MS); M;
M (from MS)
66-67   EEO (from MS)
68   RB
69   PV
70-71   HE
72   Ontario Place
73   Bill McKay
(from MS)
74-75   GH
76-77   EEO (from MS)
78   GH; M
79   Gordon Reeve
80-81   Ontario Department
Tourism and
Information
82   JDV; PV; JDV; JDV;
Ontario Department
of Highways
83   BD; BD; JDV; JDV;
JDV; JDV
86-87   JDV
88-89   M
90   M
91   HE
92   HE
93   M

94   RB
95   RB
96   JDV
97   JDV; M
98   M; PB
99   M
100-101   PV
104-105   JDV
106-107   PV; PV
108   PB
109   PB
110   JL
111   PV
112-113   Don Newlands
114   Rolly Ford
(from MS)
115   JL
116   JL
117   Chris Bruun
(from MS)
118-119   VREB-Czolowski
120   JL
121   JL
122   M
123   Mike Dobel
(from MS)
124   MD (from MS)
125   DN
126   DN
127   Gerald Campbell

Typeset in Canada/Printed in Italy/Bound in Canada